M000078180

Country Living
is Risky Business

by Nick &
Anita Evangelista

Loompanics Unlimited
Port Townsend, Washington

Neither the author nor the publisher assumes any responsibility for the use or misuse of information contained in this book. It is sold for entertainment purposes only. Be Warned!

Country Living is Risky Business
© 2000 by Nick & Anita Evangelista

Published by:
Loompanics Unlimited
PO Box 1197
Port Townsend, WA 98368
Loompanics Unlimited is a division of Loompanics Enterprises, Inc.
Phone: 360-385-2230
E-mail: service@loompanics.com
Web site: www.loompanics.com

Cover Design by Shary Flenniken

ISBN 1-55950-193-6
Library of Congress Card Catalog Number 00-106167

Contents

Section One
Getting Started

Section Two
Animals and Livestock

Section Three
Wrapping It Up

Epilogue

Those who will, the gods lead; those who won't, they drag.
— Roman proverb

Adventure is never fun while you're having it.
— Rule of Thumb

Dedication

To
Sir James ("River Kwai") Garrett
and Dame Suzette Garrett,
and Sean and Justin:

Hope you're satisfied, Jim!

Introduction

There are no dinosaurs in this book — unless you consider chickens dinosaurs. We sometimes do. There are no car chases: it's hard to speed when your vehicle is loaded down with bales of hay. There are no robots from the future, no pirates, no hunts for lost treasures, and no psycho killers — unless you consider goats psycho killers. We most certainly do all the time.

Within these pages you will not find the overtly spectacular, the earth-shaking, or the illicit. Sorry.

So, you might ponder, No robots? No psychos? No sex? How could a book without androids, knife-wielding loonies, or at least one steamy grope be worth reading? Why should I bother with a book that's admittedly bereft of all the liveliest material of our literary age?

Well, do you like personal challenge, self-reliance, nature in all its unrelenting aggressiveness? In short, reality unpaved and unpolished.

That's what this book has to offer.

Experience.

Life.

But not comfortable life with its rules and cushions, or some kind of vicarious "lifestyle of the rich and famous."

We mean, LIFE.

A dynamic process.

This is a life that's attainable, affordable, and there for the taking. But it is gritty, barnyardy, bone-bruising, hit-the-wall stuff. With a few laughs thrown in. You just pick your poison (metaphorically-speaking), grab it tight, and hold on 'til the rope stops flopping. Even with all the angst, there's something to be said for being able to look back on your experiences and say, "I did that!"

Is this worth reading about?

All mine.
(Photo credit: Justin Evangelista)

We promise everything in this book is true. We lived it and learned it. A couple names have been changed to protect the extremely guilty, but that's about it for stretching veracity.

We didn't have to make anything up, because we've been "blessed" in our life with a direct line to the Universe's Department of the Bizarre. Maybe not space alien, *X-Files* bizarre, but certainly out of kilter with the nine-to-five world. This has given us many life lessons to write about.

� ✕ ✕ ✕ ✕ ✕

The following is another ample sampling of the good and not so good things that have happened to us since we fled Los Angeles in 1985. Also, of course, are many bits of info we've collected along the way.

Finally, we hope you enjoy reading what we have to say. If you do, you'll certainly have a better time than we sometimes did living it. If it ends up making you want to move to a farm in some out of the way rural place, good for you! But don't blame us.

Best wishes.

And good luck!

Section One
Getting Started

Chapter One
Nothing New

"There is a tide in the affairs of men
Which, taken at the flood, leads on to fortune:
Omitted, all the voyage of their life
Is bound in shallows and miseries"
— Shakespeare, Julius Caesar, IV, iii

Comings and Goings of the
"Back-to-the-Land" Movement

In 1970, a young writer and fledgling farmer put together a newsletter to keep in touch with other people who had interests similar to his own: "organic" gardening, the troubles in the national economy, raising livestock on a small scale, solar power, living "close to the earth," living as economically as possible, avoiding the 9-to-5 grind, communal living, and spiritual development. The first issue was published on cheap newsprint, since the young man was what we would call "poor, but resourceful." It was a slim handful of pages without illustrations — just a couple articles, some thoughts, some ideas. Distributed by mail-order through classified advertisements, and by hand to local shops, it looked like it was destined to be just one newsletter among many that dealt with alternative lifestyles. John Shuttleworth called his newsletter, *The Mother Earth News.*

Fifteen years later, John Shuttleworth sold The Mother Earth News *empire* — including the cutting edge magazine, acres of property, solar homes, gardens, and alternative centers — for some undisclosed *millions* of dollars.

What happened was this: *The Mother Earth News* (TMEN) became the voice for a growing movement — the heart and

8

soul of the 1970's "back-to-the-landers" (BTTLs). There were competitors with their own angles, such as jd Belanger's *Countryside Magazine* and Lynn Miller's *Practical Horse-farming* and *Small Farmer's Journal* (later known simply as *Small Farmer's Journal*) — but *TMEN* remained in the forefront.

We can look at this from fifty different angles — good management, picking up a trend, foresight, luck, careful investment, etc., etc., etc., — but the most important part of *TMEN's* success was one thing: the back-to-the-land movement.

When Shuttleworth rolled out his little newsletter, it happened to be at the very beginning of a remarkable, recurring, and consistent population trend, a trend that has taken place like clockwork every twenty-to-thirty years or so in the twentieth century — going back still earlier into the nineteenth century, too. As a reader of this book, you're riding the crest of the latest wave of BTTLs — as you'll see, it is a grand tradition, steeped in history, but destined to repeat the same steps as our forebears.

Major Tides

When the two of us came onto the tail end of the last great BTTL movement of 1973-83 (some say, 1975-85, but what's the point of quibbling?), we did so with the near stereotypical behavior of someone from that era: we moved from a deep urban area (Los Angeles) to a deep rural region (the Ozarks). We moved in our VW van — as stereotypical a vehicle as there was for that movement in that time period. We moved with astonishing ignorance about what we were getting into — but with equally astonishing confidence that we could meet and beat any challenges that came our way. We weren't hippies, though... more like innocent proto-intellectuals/spiritual-seekers/earnest young parents/organic growers/animal lovers/environmentalists/political rebels/and maybe, just maybe, junior adventurers. We knew, *for sure*, that we were doing the **right** thing.

So did Betty MacDonald's husband — but he made his move in the late WWII years, dragging his doubtful writer-wife along on the trip. Betty MacDonald wrote about her BTTL horrors in the best-selling humor book, *The Egg and I* (later made into a 1947 Fred McMurray/Claudette Colbert film with the same name). Funny thing was that *every trauma she encountered we ALSO experienced:* broken down house, "cultural collision," needing help from the rural neighbors, problems with livestock, trying to learn from books, having to do everything on their own, fighting the elements — the details were different, but the essentials were the same. The book was written at the beginning of the great post-War BTTL movement, fueled by GIs returning from overseas with confidence and hunger for safety and security — about 1947-55, give or take a couple years.

As early as 1942, though, the trend was already underway — we can see its glimmerings in the popular Bing Crosby and Fred Astaire film, *Holiday Inn*. Crosby plays a performer who is tired of the hustle and bustle of theatrical life — he buys a Vermont farm, and struggles in humorous episodes with livestock, keeping warm, house repair, canning fruits, and trying to learn to plow (with a horse!) — but gives it up in frustration. After resting up at a "sanitarium," he opens an inn at the farm... life is all singing and dancing after that.

Holiday Inn actually had its roots in an **earlier** BTTL movement, the one that gave a voice to a former professor and his student-wife, Scott and Helen Nearing. The Nearings were clearly the spiritual-parents of the 70s-80s BTTL movement even though their experience was already 35 years old by then; their books are still available today. Both Nearings left "civilization" for deep rural New England — driven by their sympathies with the "worker's movement" (closely allied with the Communist movement at the time), troubled by the power the government was wielding over the populace, worried that the economy was self-destructing, politically opposed to meat-eating and domestication of animals — they represented the classical "intellectual" BTTLers who sought to create their own little corner of nirvana in the wild woods.

Just *exactly* like today's BTTLers, and the post-WWII BTTLers, the Nearings moved from their well-paid city employment out to the farm-country. They built their own home from the materials at hand, learned about country living *by doing*, made their fair share of mistakes, and lived to not only tell about it, but to find peace in their chosen simple lifestyle. It probably helped that when they bought their property, it could be had (literally) for a few dollars an acre... now, the entire area is prime winter vacation country and you can't touch property even with a bankroll big enough to choke a cow.

The Nearings (along with Maurice Kains, author of *Five Acres and Independence*, 1935), represented only the most vocal tip of the BTTL iceberg at that time, though, as city-folks fled joblessness and the growing financial depression for grandma's farm. There was a tide, but the advent of WWII pulled the BTTLers and everyone else away from their goals.

Earlier Still

A little before 1915, American farming was at its profitable height. A family could buy quality rural land, crop it, and pay off the mortgage in 3-5 years from the proceeds... everything grown or manufactured on the farm after that was "pure profit." We, of the early 21st century — who think that a home takes 30 years to pay off — can hardly understand the sense of freedom, of self-reliance, or of security that kind of circumstance would create!

But there was a mini-BTTL movement just before 1915, generated by the phenomenal period of social confidence that took place after the turn of the 20th century. Why, there were phones, and cooking gas, and horseless carriages, and telegraphs, and electricity, and man was learning to fly! Anything you wanted, anything at all, could be ordered from a catalog and shipped right to the nearest post office — the same kind of convenience as we have today with the Internet. America under Teddy Roosevelt was potent, a power to be reckoned with, and just beginning to stretch her wings. Surely, peace and prosperity would go on forever!

At the start of WWI, "over there" and "not over here," young couples looked to the cheap farmland, made their decisions, and moved. By 1915, an economic downturn — perhaps caused by the "over there" war — brought a wave of farm losses and foreclosures... and that mini-BTTL movement stalled.

Aside from the cheap land and booming farm economy, what spurred those early BTTLers? Part of the credit can go to a series of periodicals from another BTTL movement, the great 1880-1890s "Golden Age of American Agriculture." These periodicals included *The American Agriculturalist*; *The Prairie Farmer, A Weekly Journal for The Farm, Orchard and Fireside* (later called *The Orange Judd Farmer*); *The Cultivator and Country Gentleman*; *Wallace's Farmer and Dairyman*; and even *The Nebraska Farmer*.

The Orange Judd Farmer, ("Orange Judd" was the editor's name) an excellent example of the mindset of that time period, was subtitled: *"Dedicated to Farming; to Live Stock of all Kinds; to Dairying; Markets; to Horticulture in all its Branches; to Housekeeping; to the Young."* This was a maga-

zine for everyone on the farm, for the "country gentleman" —
who is our equivalent of an educated BTTLer who operates a
non-farm business off the farm — and for the wife and kid-
dies, as well.

What is most amazing about all of these publications is that
the very same articles, issues, and discussions that appear
there, *are still being discussed* in modern issues of *Backwoods
Home*, *Countryside*, and *Small Farmer's Journal*, among other
current periodicals. From "how-to's" (raising chickens, getting
eggs in winter, feeding hogs, making a profit, baking bread,
using equipment, building a shed, games for kids, and so
forth) to technical pieces (breed characteristics, profiles, "new
product," and home inventions), they thought, and worried,
and planned, and wrote the same things we BTTLers do today.

For instance, in an 1888 issue of *American Agriculturalist*,
one reader sent in his suggestion on "marketing apples."
George B. Arnold wrote that his orchard was just beginning to
bear fruit:

> "My plan is to assort my fruit into four grades — extra,
> first, second, and culls. The extras must contain only the very
> choicest specimens and be put up in smaller packages than
> the first or No. 1 which will be put up in full standard sized
> packages and will contain nothing but fair sound fruit of uni-
> form size, as near as may be, and always graded up to the
> same standard, marked accordingly, and shipped to reliable
> commission men [middlemen wholesalers — Ed.]. The third
> grade, or No. 2, will be good, sound fruit that is not up to the
> standard of No. 1, and will go to the evaporator ["drier" for
> dried fruit — Ed.], while the culls will go to the cider press
> and then into vinegar. By a strict, uniform system of grading
> and packing, I am not ashamed to have my name appear on
> the package."

Not only is Mr. Arnold's plan sound and still perfectly applicable today, it *could have been written today...* marketing apples is virtually the same now as then.

Another issue of the same magazine, also from 1888, carried an article that we'd call a "profile" today — it discussed a Mr. S.L. Bedson, who was raising and breeding "beefalos" — crosses of buffalo and beef cattle. Like a current magazine, the article discussed a little of the background of bison, the hay that was fed to the animals in winter, the characteristics of the herd ("An old buffalo cow has an evil eye at any time..."), and the profitability of the specimens. Aside from the use of the language, the article could appear in any number of "small farm" publications — with the same sense of newness and excitement — *right now.*

This was the "Golden Age" of American agriculture, all right — farmers owned their land, made and sold their own farm inventions, bred and improved their livestock using the newly discovered ideas about genetics, and relied on their own skills and strength when something went awry. Taxes were minute, compared to today; no federal government or state government bureaucracy to determine how much corn you could or couldn't grow; no laws restricted how you used your own land. BTTLers invested their savings from city jobs, did wisely and well, and became the "gentlemen farmers" they dreamed of becoming — and BTTLers took their money, made poor choices, failed to make a go of it, and ended up back in the city trying to find work. *The same as today.*

Still further back in time, a young single man — maybe comparable to an idealistic, artistic hippie of the 1970s, maybe a lot like one of the seekers of the 1930s — moved from his tiresome city life as a magazine editor out to a little one-room cabin beside a pond. During the day, he chopped kindling for his stove, grew a small garden, walked through the woods appreciating nature, and wrote copious notes about his experiences. In the evening, he visited some farming neighbors, charmed them with his conversation, and chowed down their generous meals. He lived in this bucolic fashion — basically a non-paying indolent guest on someone else's property — for two years, two months, two days. In 1854, he collected his writing and *Walden* was published. Henry David Thoreau spent the rest of his life writing, traveling, and working at his family's pencil business, dying of tuberculosis in 1862. He missed most of the excitement of the War Between the States — even though his entire era was permeated by the social troubles that led up to that conflagration.

People read Thoreau's classic, and said to themselves, "If that city boy can live so peacefully among nature, so can I" — so Thoreau can truly be said to be the "Father of the BTTL Movement" from the 19th century onward into the 1980s. Unfortunately, those readers "forgot" that Thoreau never had to harvest a hay crop, prepare a dinner, or make a mortgage payment — and trying to imitate Thoreau's life would be a quick trip to the bankruptcy court.

Nevertheless, the image of country life as one beautiful, serene, thoughtful sermon, lived against a backdrop of quiet sensual joy and refinement, has stuck with us, thanks to Thoreau. Thoreau, by the way, only *observed* cows. He never dirtied his hands trying to actually *milk* one.

Even so...

Thoreau wasn't the beginning of BTTLs, and wasn't even the middle. Every time we start to think that we've found something "new" by moving BTTL, we're reminded of the great Roman General and politician, Marcus Portius Cato.

Cato led a long, illustrious life (234 BC to 149 BC) — a moral and physical spartan during Rome's own Golden Age of

Agriculture, even as the empire was at the leading edge of its long decline. After putting in his time as a soldier, general, politician, orator, and all-around temperance-advocate, he packed up his family and moved out to his farm. From there, this BTTLer wrote a volume on agriculture, wrote his city friends and begged them to come see his "glorious cabbages," boiled his own "delicate and esteemed" turnips while his wife baked bread, and even brought a toga-load of fat brown figs into town and dropped them on the Senate floor — to the admiration of all the politicians present! Of course, it probably helped this early BTTLer that Cato had a household full of slaves to do the boring garden work, like hoeing and weed-pulling.

Over and over, it's the same story, repeated from as early as humankind had cities and a way to record the data — city dwellers find reasons to move out to the country. This is so consistent a theme, worldwide, that we have to believe there is something innate in people that calls us back to our native roots — and something inherently wrong or primally unfulfilling about the concrete jungle that drives some of the best and brightest away to seek "something else" in the boondocks.

BTTL Cycles

Thanks to the furor over Y2K, an entire segment of society that had *no* interest in rural living woke up one day and said, "What if there is no electricity, no trucks to ship food or goods, no oil for transportation or for farming, thanks to the failure of our computer-dependent infrastructure?" That question revealed some deep-seated fundamental weaknesses in the way our society functions, and how our singular dependence upon fragile computer links and interlinks left us open to potentially terrible and deadly disruptions.

But, Y2K "didn't happen." At least, not as the chicken littles thought it would. The early months of 2000 showed numerous failures in water pumping, chemical plants, oil refining, nuclear power stations, accounting, record keeping, and aircraft — but not enough to stop the vast engine of our economy. Crude oil, alone, doubled in price within the first two months of the year — maybe something really *was* going on with the refining plants... maybe... just enough to make alert people aware that "something" wasn't right anymore (if it ever had been). Just enough to trigger the spark for the next BTTL movement.

The astute reader may have already noticed that three of the great BTTL movements in the 20th century came during times of great social crisis: the depression of the 1930s, the post-WWII recession and rebuilding, and the moral upheaval following the Vietnam era. Thoreau's bucolic adventures prefaced the Civil War, and took place when the country was in a moral and political turmoil. Even the glorious Golden Age was marred by a drive to make the world an American empire — by killing Filipinos and Spaniards in overseas wars.

If we look further back through the Golden Age and all the way to Thoreau (with the exception of the stalled BTTL movment of 1915), we find another interesting pattern: the rationale that drove each BTTL movement was either "spiritually" oriented, or "practically" oriented, more or less. While no BTTL movement was exclusively "spiritual" or "practical," let's look at their features.

Thoreau (circa 1850-60s): **spiritual**, including vegetarianism, pastoralism, "natural foods," communing with nature, sense of "higher calling"... favorite of intellectuals and the educated.

Golden Age (circa 1880-90s): **practical**, including livestock breeding, farm management, home improvement, meat consumption, focus on profits... preferred by middle-class hands-on types.

Nearing/Depression (circa 1920-30s): **spiritual**, primarily, with vegetarianism, political and economic concerns, natural foods, "higher calling"... educated intellectuals, politically disaffected. Subgroup of "practicals" who moved temporarily due to financial concerns (Kains-type).

Post-WWII (circa 1945-55s): **practical**, seeking quiet life that also returned a good profit, meat consuming... high-energy former GIs with hands-on skill and willingness to work (middle and lower classes).

Vietnam era (circa 1970s-80s): **spiritual**, "back-to-the-land" nature seekers, vegetarian, natural foods, "higher calling," politically disaffected... educated and intellectuals.

Now, if there's anything at all to cycles in nature or human behavior, it's pretty clear that the next BTTL movement in this series "should" be a "practical" movement, one that has at its foundation a healthy urge to work hard, live in "better" surroundings than urbia/suburbia can offer, that is fueled by middle-class hands-on types, and is characterized less by "escape to nature" than by "optimism to build."

While the Golden Age "practical" BTTL movement was buoyed by new developments in genetics and animal breeding, and the post-WWII move was fueled by self-assured GIs in a constricting economy — what might power the Next Great BTTL movement?

The Next Great BTTL Movement

No BTTL movement begins or flourishes in a social vacuum; they all have a context and continuity with the cultural setting, problems, beliefs, and stresses.

18

Computers will be a major part of the next BTTL movement — first, in setting the stage through Y2K concerns that computers possess socially deadly flaws that could crack at any moment. Second, computers will fuel this BTTL movement *because* they are changing the texture of our culture: for a small, alert segment, computers and the Internet are now the primary news media (with instantaneous reports from events everywhere in the world), the primary business "machine," the primary investment "tool" (especially for day-traders), the primary educational and research resource, and a marvelous way to earn an income at a distance from the main business.

The economy will fire the next BTTL movement — either by blowing through the roof on its way to the stratosphere, or by hitting the ceiling and crashing unceremoniously back to reality. Either direction will produce a shocking change in society — if the economy goes up, more money, more investments, more development, more stuff for all, then a percentage of people who are put off by the increased "service" cubicle-drone labor go ahead and work up their gumption and break away. It's not that they dislike money or the social structure, it's just that they can't stand the pointlessness of their own work — they'll be seeking hands-on *purposeful* work where they can see the results of their labors. They'll bring a lot of their interests with them, such as a desire for good restaurants, fine wine, art, literature, and live entertainment.

If the economy tanks, cubicle-drones will find themselves out-of-work — in an economy that gives them *no opportunities*. These are the young Gen-Xers, who have *never known* an economic downturn, *never known* a lack of goods or services, *never known* a sense of social hopelessness and helplessness. Here are the people who awaken one morning and realize the life they have believed would go on forever was a lie — and then, they will look for a truly "eternal" lifestyle, the one their ancestors lived on the farm. But, with a computer, good TV reception, and access to theaters!

Oil may be one reason for the coming BTTL movement. According to various industry sources, the world reached its maximum oil pumping and refining capacity in 1995... it's going downhill from there, with little hope for an upward change. Oil is the lubrication for our infrastructure machinery, for the economy, for our capacity to build and expand. Without oil, for trucks, cars, jets, railroads, transportation will slow to a fraction of what is possible at the turn of this century — and the place you live will take on a stunning importance. Want your kids to go to school in a small classroom with lots of teacher attention? Pick either an expensive private city school just around the corner, or a small town/rural public school down the road — your kids can walk to either one, if there aren't any oil-gulping busses running.

Population changes will affect the next BTTL movement, too. While rabid environmentalists still say that America's 2.3 children born to each woman will cause "overpopulation," the truth is that reproduction has dropped precipitously in the US: white American women's fertility produces 1.9 births, and black American women only 2.2 — these are not the numbers that live to maturity, either. According to the UN Population Division's *1998 World Population Prospects* report, global population growth rates peaked about 1970, and have fallen steadily since then. This UN report predicts that world population will plummet between 2040 and 2050 as us oldsters begin to die off, and continue decreasing by 25% each succeeding generation.

Overseas, some European leaders are now arranging financial and political venues to *support* (that is, *give extra money to)* women who choose to actually have children! Swedish mothers get paid a stipend, have access to free childcare AND healthcare, and don't have to work — because the population is *falling*, not rising.

The same UN report states that by 2050, those who are over 65 will outnumber children 15 and younger *three to one*. Who will pay your Social Security when you are old, and there are three people your age for every one person paying into the system? Wouldn't it be nice to have a paid-for little farmette that produces all your food — and food for your grandkids — and earns a little income? *Do you think you're the only person who understands this?*

Disease, war, climate and geological changes will hasten the advent of the BTTL movement, IF they happen in a visible fashion. This will be the case because natural and biological disasters will increase the sense of insecurity of city life — if, say, your city was under a "biological warfare alert," would you think twice about staying there? How much is your job *really worth?* Is it worth possibly sacrificing your own life to a wacko terrorist who unleashes a mason jar full of anthrax in the super-mall one night? Is it worth the health or safety of your kids? A lot of people will be asking themselves these same questions while lying awake staring at the ceiling, in the deep, dark, middle of the night.

If disease, war, climate and geological changes DON'T happen in a big way, it won't stop the next BTTL movement... merely reduce the reasons people have for making that final move.

When?

Unfortunately, our crystal ball has gone dark on that one. As previously stated, we believe the concern over Y2K has set the stage for the next BTTL movement — people who would never have considered a rural lifestyle suddenly found that option *very* appealing, when considering the alternatives. People all over the country left city jobs and moved to rural areas or bought "vacation" property and outfitted it for sustainability, rapidly learned to can fruits, dry meats, purify water, raise small livestock, all because of the concern that today's cultural system ran the risk of toppling from its own ponderous weight. A lot of these people discovered that they *preferred* their simpler lifestyle and refused the "quick move back." These are the FIRST of the new wave of "practical" BTTLers.

When?

It's already starting.

Hang on to your hats!

Chapter Two
In the Beginning

Nick: I can remember the first time Anita ever brought up the subject of moving away from Los Angeles to the country. We were driving down Hollywood Boulevard in her red Mazda. It was a bright summer Saturday afternoon. We'd known each other maybe three weeks. She looked over at me innocently, "Do you think you'd ever like to live anywhere else than L.A.?" I shook my head rather energetically. "No," I said, "never. I like living here. I'll always live here. This is my home."

Well, what can I say? Wrong again! But, back then, it sure seemed definite.

The process of change was a subtle one.

It crept up on me like a virus.

❀❀❀❀❀❀

Anita: Our conversion to country people began simply enough. We put in a three-foot-by-six-foot garden in our backyard. Small. It had to start small — we lived on a claustrophobic, forty-foot-by-seventy-foot lot, and that included the house and garage. It seemed like a big garden at the time — tomatoes, and lettuce and peas and a green pepper plant — it was like a miniature Eden, producing year-around in that mild climate.

We read books. We subscribed to magazines that dealt with farm life, organic gardening, self-reliance, conservation, and ecology — all kinds of non-city stuff. We thought we were radicals. Our relatives *knew* we were. Then, we expanded our operation.

We put in dwarf fruit trees (four) in both the back and front yards. We built a raised strawberry patch by our front porch. We set grape plants up against the house. We planted all kinds of exotic flowers.

As our projects came to life, as plants almost magically appeared where there'd only been dirt, as trees blossomed and fruit took shape, we suddenly felt connected to the world.

Nature became accessible.

❈ ❈ ❈ ❈ ❈ ❈

Nick: Then, we went nuts. We bought livestock. We lived ten minutes from downtown L.A., and we were buying farm animals — chickens, rabbits, quail, that kind of thing. Plus, we had five big dogs and maybe 15 or 20 neighborhood cats hung out around the house.

When people asked me why, I told them sunspots made us do it. We *must* have been crazy. The kinds of regulations we were bucking — health, animal regulation, sanitation disposal, business, zoning — I can only imagine. We never checked. If we had, we probably would have been too horrified to ever get going, much less succeed.

To start with, Anita got seven rabbits — five does and two bucks — from a person she found in the newspaper classifieds.

Not surprisingly, our rabbits multiplied. Rapidly. We sold babies to a local pet store. We did especially well at Easter.

Our bunnies were always the healthiest ones they had for sale, the owner told us, and he paid us top price for them — $3 each.

We built more cages. Before long, we had twenty female breeders and two males. They more than paid for themselves. Also, the rabbit manure went straight into our gardens. I'm glad it had some place to go. There was an awful lot of it.

✖✖✖✖✖✖

Anita: Next, we added chickens, mostly for eggs. We ended up with so many eggs, we had to give them away to friends and acquaintances and relatives. Why we didn't think of selling them, I can't imagine.

We had Rhode Island Reds, Barred Rocks, Cornish, Leghorns, Minorcas, Cochins, Anconas, Fayoumis, Hamburgs, Polish, Brahmas, and one Japanese silkie (which we called our ornamental chicken, as she never laid one egg).

The chickens had a large pen to move around in out behind our garage. We lined it with alfalfa hay we purchased from a distant horse stable — a single bale cost $10. That gave the chickens something to scratch around in, making them as happy as chickens probably get.

Unfortunately, putting in alfalfa hay instead of, say, straw hay, led to problems — giving us our first taste of the realities of farm life.

The first time it rained, the hay got really soaked.

Then, it started to smell. The books didn't say what to do about this, so — thinking like newbies — we covered it over with fresh hay. This seemed to do the trick, so every time it rained — which in L.A. wasn't all that often — we repeated the procedure. It wasn't all that long before the chickens were bouncing around on a thick carpet of old, intensely smelly, hay.

I remember the morning I walked out in the back yard and was suddenly assaulted by this, shall we say, odor. It struck me in the face like a falling slab of freeway concrete in an earthquake. It was awful. Actually, the word "awful" makes it sound a lot nicer than it was. It wasn't difficult to track down the cause.

The chicken yard.

Rotting alfalfa plus chicken droppings plus uneaten chicken feed plus moisture equaled the smell of the living dead. The chickens didn't seem to mind, but we didn't much like it.

Two days later, my mother showed up on our front porch with the disquieting message that neighbors had mentioned that a rather unpleasant aroma seemed to be wafting unhappily from our property.

There was only one thing to do. Nick had to start cleaning out the chicken pen.

✼✼✼✼✼✼

Nick: I cleaned the chicken pen by hand. Tools? Pitchfork? Huh? What's that? We were slow learners.

I began peeling away layers of compacted hay. Halfway down, I reached the slime level. Under that was bug metropolis. Then, came the methane, which had been pretty well trapped beneath this decomposing mess. I think there was enough methane gas trapped here to run the world for a century or two. Thick, billowing clouds came up to greet me with every newly exposed section of ground. But it wasn't wasted. I got to breathe in a good portion of the vapor, which made the inside of my head feel real unusual, like there was enough room behind my eyes to hold marathon bicycle races.

Anyway, I removed all this muck. Over two thousand smelly pounds of it (it seemed like). That stuff really held in the moisture. I put it in trash bags, and set it out at the curb for the trash folks to cart away. Hey, it was organic.

Then, we started all over again with fresh, bright alfalfa hay. Only the best for our hens!

Aggggggggggg!

✖✖✖✖✖✖

Anita: During a visit to the Los Angeles County Fair — Nick and I were real farmer people now — we added coturnix quail to our menagerie. Six of them. Putting a newly purchased incubator to use, we took the eggs we got and hatched them.

Before we knew it, we had over a hundred quail. They grew fast. And were they ever noisy. And mean. I remember one unlucky quail that was attacked for no reason in particular by its comrades. When we found it, they'd excavated a gaping hole in its head, right down into its brain.

We were sure the bird was going to die — for Pete's sake, they'd pecked away feathers, skin, skull, one eye, and were poking into its visible brain. To our surprise, it didn't.

We put it in a cage by itself, and, day after day, small improvements took place. Skin, bone, and feathers covered the area — no new eye, though. The strangest thing of all was that even with a big chunk of its brain missing, the quail didn't act any differently. It seemed fine. While this says a lot for quail heartiness, I guess it doesn't exactly sing praises for quail intellectual skills.

✖✖✖✖✖✖

Nick: We bought some ducks. But that was a big mistake. As babies they were okay, but as soon as they grew up, they filthied up everything. There were flies everywhere. They needed standing water to swim in, and it always looked like gruel no matter how often we changed it. I could never figure out why we had ducks in the first place.

Those, we gave away.

✖✖✖✖✖✖

Anita: I forget where we found our Guinea fowl. Pearl guineas. They never got into trouble. Awful noisy, though. And eggs only in the spring.

✖✖✖✖✖✖

Nick: Anita wanted to buy a dwarf goat, but that's where I drew the line. Somehow, bringing a goat to our house seemed like spitting in church.

Anita: Just one doe, maybe a Nigerian Dwarf, would have fit right in (with a shoehorn, maybe). Just imagine! A quart of fresh, wholesome, natural goat's milk every day! In the city! The neighbors would never know — hey, goats don't make noises, do they?

✖✖✖✖✖✖

Nick: Somewhere along the line, while this animal juggling act was being played out, another element was added to the farm equation. Anita started saying, "Wouldn't it be kind of nice to live in the country?" This is how it always begins. Slowly, insidiously.

It seemed like a pleasant daydream. Maybe after we retired, in forty years or so, we would do just that — move to a pretty little cottage in the country. Keep a couple of hens, and some cats or something.

Chapter Two
In the Beginning

Before I knew what hit me, I was buried under an avalanche of "We gotta move, we gotta move, we gotta move, we gotta move, we gotta move!"

It turned into a mania. She read in *Mother Earth News* about weirdos who moved to the country and lived in cabins made out of chunks of fire wood held together with dried mud, or old barns, or teepees, and even — this one made my skin crawl — sod huts.

During a moment of extreme dementia, Anita suggested we buy a piece of land somewhere, anywhere, and live in our VW van. Even as an unexplored possibility, this did not seem like a good idea to me. At the very least, I saw us ax murdering each other after about three days exposure to this particular mode of existence. I declined. Sometimes loudly.

But Anita never let up. "Move! Move! Move!" She pounded away. Think of any of Mohammed Ali's early heavyweight championship fights, and you'll understand her tactics.

❊❊❊❊❊❊

Anita: It helps when you know you're right.

❊❊❊❊❊❊

Nick: After a bit, the idea of moving began to sink in. Thinking about the way things were going in the city — the cost of living, crime, pollution, stifling rules and regulations — I wavered noticeably. The kids were at the age where school was going to be a consideration... and home schooling was talked about.

I found myself agreeing. Yes, it was time to move. I began looking forward to the very real possibility of leaving the city behind us.

30

We sent away for real estate catalogues from around the United States. We familiarized ourselves with locations, prices, all that moving stuff.

When the day arrived to go searching for a home somewhere in rural America, we were both ready.

It took ten years to get from that first harmless sunny cruise down Hollywood Boulevard to our farm in the Ozark Mountains.

❈❈❈❈❈❈

By the way, we're sure our neighborhood threw a victory party the day we moved away.

Chapter Three
On the Farm at Last

Nick: For every city human moving to the country, there is that first day when glimmering illusion runs headlong into icy cold, hard fact. Quite often, it is a day of extreme personal trauma.

Ours was June 3, 1985. 4:30 p.m.

Cramped and definitely crabby, Anita and I, plus two small kids (one girl, one boy), a grandmother, and a large reddish-orange dog of mixed collie parentage, gazed out from the parked moving van that had been our home for three and a half days. The object of our attention was the ten acre Missouri Ozarks farm we now owned. A life in Los Angeles was behind us. A new existence lay directly ahead.

"Well, here we are," I said.

Everyone piled out of the truck like a load of old apples spilling from a ripped bag.

"What do you think?" I asked my wife, motioning proudly at the white, two-story farm house before us, the house I'd bought for us three months before, the first house we ever owned.

Anita frowned.

"It doesn't look like it did in the video you made when you were here in March," she said tentatively. "It looks... smaller." She paused. "But it's nice. It really is."

No overpopulation problem here!
(Photo credit: Justin Evangelista)

I sagged a bit. "Ah."

My five-year-old daughter Jamie pulled on my hand.

"When are we going home?" she asked.

My grandmother, who was forgetful, punched my arm.

"I don't know who you are," she declared, "but I'll have you put in jail for a thousand years for kidnapping me."

I stared at the ragged knee-high grass we were standing in. "It does look a bit different even from what I remember," I admitted, sighing.

An auspicious beginning to our back-to-the-land adventure, if ever there was one! Reality had descended. I could hear the moist thud resounding through the countryside. We were actually in Missouri. In the Ozark Mountains. On our farm. The nearest town was sixteen miles away. It was no longer a dream. We were done with theories. With speculation. With fantasies. For better or worse, this was it.

We hovered there dumbly, struck senseless and numb by the overwhelming vastness of the occasion.

After a minute or two, I broke the oppressive silence.

"What do we do now?" I said.

Anita smiled hopefully. "Why don't we look around?"

"Good idea. The place belongs to us."

"It really does, doesn't it?"

I nodded. "So is it inside first or outside?"

"Inside. That's where we're going to be living."

I laughed. "At least until knocking around out here turns us into hillbillies. Then I think we have to go bunk in the barn, and turn the house into a chicken coop, or something. That's what they did in Ma and Pa Kettle movies and *Snuffy Smith* comics."

"That kind of thing doesn't really happen," Anita said.

"You want to bet? Didn't you ever see *Lord of the Flies*? Some kids get stranded on a desert island and — whammo! — they turn into —"

"Hillbillies?"

"No, no, no! They turn into little, bloodthirsty savages."

"You think living close to Nature will turn us into savages?"

"Not exactly. Maybe 'Lords of the Goats.' We'll end up eating corn pone — whatever *that* is — and brewing whiskey in a still out behind the wood shed. Pigs'll sleep in our bathtub. I'll change my name legally to 'Jethro'."

"Forget it, buddy. We're not that far out in the wilderness."

"Oh yeah? I think I saw the name 'Big Foot' on one of the mail boxes we passed on our way out here."

Anita eyed me.

"Go inside. You've obviously had too much sun."

We headed for the back door, along the right side of the house. It was the only door that came with a key.

Anita stopped as she passed by a window. "Isn't that dry rot?"

I poked my finger into brittle, crumbly wood. The window frame was pretty much shot.

"It looks like dry rot," I said. "I didn't notice that before."

"No one does," Anita pointed out. "You never see the flaws when you buy a house. It's a cosmic law of the universe. If most people actually saw what they were in the process of buying, they'd have themselves checked into a psych ward."

I stared. "I bought a house that needs a dermatologist."

Anita shrugged. "I guess we have some renovating ahead of us."

"That's just fine," I groaned. "Like we don't have anything else do to around here."

I felt the weight of unforeseen burdens crashing down upon my shoulders. Ah! The joys of home ownership.

We arrived at the back door. I pulled out the key our realtor had mailed to us in California.

"I hope this thing fits in the lock," I said. "Because it's the only one we have."

Mercifully, the key slipped into the lock. The door swung open with a sharp moan, as if to say, "People! Here we go again."

Wasps, unexpectedly interrupted in their mud nest building, dive-bombed us with angry insistence.

"I hate wasps!" Anita snapped, ducking her head.

"The house has been empty for over two years," I reminded her.

"I'm allergic to stings!"

"Okay, okay. We'll buy some insect spray in town tomorrow, and we'll nuke every one of the little creeps. Now, let's just go on in. Kids, come on in the house, guys. Grab Gram before she escapes. Everyone watch out for killer bugs."

"You'll get the chair for this," my grandmother insisted. "I told the governor about you."

"Fine," I said. "If you just come along quietly, I promise I'll turn myself in after dinner."

"Maybe they'll let you off with a good beating," Anita remarked.

We found ourselves in the kitchen. The room was hot and stuffy. The air smelled like mold, like somebody else's home. Crispy, long deceased insects littered the white and blue linoleum floor. One wall was covered with gray stone slabs, the others with rustic, brown paneling. I'd liked the paneling the first time I saw it.

"Paneling," Anita announced.

"I kind of like it," I said.

"Unsanitary. It's got to go."

"Huh?" I said. "Well, let's look at the other rooms."

Large, unnamed black bugs scuttled for cover as we wandered through our home. We walked slowly, quietly absorbing the uniqueness of everything.

We were upstairs counting spider webs when we heard a vehicle pull up in front of the house.

"Who could that be?" Anita wondered.

"Burglars? Jehovah's Witnesses? Space Aliens?"

"Maybe you should look."

I bounced down the stairway and threw open the front door. It was our realtor, Ed, in his enormous red pickup. Ed, looking like a massive potato in a short-sleeved shirt and slacks, lurched out of his truck and shuffled up the walkway toward me.

"I think I just ran over your dog," he proclaimed, as he stepped on to the front porch.

Some greeting.

I looked out on to the road. There was indeed a very dead brown dog. It wasn't ours, though. Wonderful, I thought. What a creative method of introducing ourselves to our neighbors. "Hi, we just moved in down the road. And, by the way, we just killed your pet. Sorry. We're the Manson family."

"I'd clean that up pretty fast, if I were you," Ed advised. "You know. The heat and all."

My mouth hanging open, I nodded dully. This is not happening, I told myself. I'm still in Los Angeles, and I'm sound asleep. I'm dreaming. Badly.

Ed's nose bobbed up and down as he spoke.

"Anyway, I just thought I'd be the first to welcome you to the Ozarks."

"You have done that, Ed. I'll never forget this moment."

"Makes you feel at home, doesn't it?"

"Oh yes."

Anita came out on the porch.

"I heard voices."

"It's Ed, our realtor," I said.

He clamped a stubby-fingered paw over Anita's hand, crushing it.

"So, this is the missus," he chuckled, oblivious to my wife's grimacing face. Ed carried his own world like a cheap suitcase. "I'm Ed." He ambled out on to our front lawn.

Anita shook her fused fingers and looked at me.

"You bought a house from this man?" she mumbled.

I shrugged.

Ed took a deep breath.

"I sold you folks a real nice house," he announced.

We nodded.

"You got yourselves some view, too."

Ed stared out over the wooded hills and sloping fields that surrounded us in a gentle grip of green.

I leaned close to Anita.

"When he gets ready to drive away," I whispered, "don't you or the kids stand near his truck."

"Why?"

"I'll explain later. For now, just don't."

Abruptly, Ed began clawing at his right leg with vigorous abandon.

"I think I picked me up some chiggers," he exclaimed.

"Chiggers?" Anita said.

"You don't know about chiggers?"

"No."

"Why, I thought everybody knew about them. Chiggers is itty-bitty bugs. You can't see them, but you sure can feel them when they start eating you up. They burrow right into your skin. And what an itch. You just want to keep scratching until you hit bone. You'll know what I mean in a day or two."

"Something to look forward to," I remarked.

"Yep," Ed grinned.

I changed the subject. "So, you think we got a deal with this place?"

Ed nodded, scratching his other leg. "Yes, I do. This is one dandy farm. It's a shame the last two families that owned it couldn't appreciate it."

"How's that?" Anita asked.

Ed ran a hand through his very much greased-down hair.

"Oh, you know, city people. They couldn't take living out here in the country. The first ones drank a lot, and ended up in bad debt. The last bunch — folks who sold the farm to you — they got a divorce. I think the wife checked into a loony farm up near St. Louis or something."

Ed missed his calling. He should have been one of those inspirational/motivational speakers.

He checked his watch.

"Oh, I guess I'd better get going," he announced. "I have a house to show in an hour."

I hoped no one there had any dogs. Ed took a few steps, then turned back.

"Did I," he asked, "mention snakes?"

"Snakes?" Anita and I echoed.

Snakes?

"Yeah," he said. "They're all over the place. This tall grass'll be perfect for 'em. And under rocks. Don't turn over any rocks. And don't reach into a space you can't see into. Might tell the kids not to go into the barns by themselves either."

"Oh?"

"Especially watch out for copperheads. Talk about poisonous. One of them buggers bites you, and you just kind of swell up like a sponge cake and die, twisting and twitching."

I glanced at Anita.

Anita glanced at me.

Belligerent vipers hiding all over our property — in the grass, in the bushes, in the trees — just waiting for the right moment to leap out and sink their dagger-like fangs into our soft, citified flesh. Vast hordes of them were out there. And the only thing they wanted, really wanted, in all the world, was to bite us. If the chiggers didn't get us first.

Ed continued.

"You stay out of tall grass unless you got high boots on — like what I'm wearing. I don't go anywhere without boots. Rattlesnakes, they love the tall grass to hide in."

Also rattlesnakes?

Now old Ed was on a roll.

"And remember about the rocks."

"Snakes hang out under rocks," I said.

Ed's eyes grew wide.

"You bet! Real nasty ones. Killers."

Apparently, the only spot we wouldn't encounter snakes was inside our refrigerator.

Any pioneer resolve that had survived our cross-country trek melted away right then and there, like a chocolate candy bar on a sweltering summer city sidewalk. Snakes! We were doomed. We weren't ready for snakes. We weren't zoned for reptiles in Los Angeles. Goats and cows and pigs and chickens and sheep, even horses, we could handle. We wanted Old MacDonald's farm, not Jurassic Park.

The cracks in our dream were widening into a major continental drift. Basically, we could never leave our house again. Our life was over.

"Thanks for the tips, Ed," I said.

"I love helping folks," Ed replied, beaming.

I'm sure, in his way, he did.

"I got to go for sure now," he declared.

We did not argue.

Climbing into his truck, Ed revved the engine wildly. He left in a cloud of choking reddish road dust, speeding past the dog in the road as though it didn't exist. For him, it probably didn't.

Anita turned to me and shook her head.

"You actually, actually bought a farm from him?" she said, repeating her earlier question.

"I was really stressed out at the time."

"Too many Twinkies. This is what I get for letting you go out by yourself."

"Well, everything has worked out okay, hasn't it?"

"You mean, this isn't the House of Usher?"

"It's a nice house — except for the dry rot, of course."

There was a long, long pause.

Anita leaned heavily against the wall, a worried expression on her face.

"Do you think we did the right thing moving here? I mean, the city was awful, but at least it was familiar. It was predictable — don't walk down dark alleys, that sort of thing. This... I don't know. I don't know how to protect the kids — or even what to be concerned about."

I shook my head. "I don't know either. I'm too tired to think right now."

"I hope we didn't make a big mistake."

40

"I guess we'll find out one way or another. I just hope when we do, it doesn't hurt too much."

Anita gave me a hug.

"This *is* it, isn't it? We're really here. On the farm. *Our* farm."

I nodded slowly.

Suddenly, Anita looked around in a panic.

"Where's the kids and your grandmother?"

I leapt off the porch at a dead run, and veered around the side of the house.

"You check the basement," I shouted. "I'll check the pond!"

Our life in the country was underway.

Chapter Four
The Worst Day of Your Life in the Country
or How to Keep on Keepin' On
41

Chapter Four
The Worst Day of Your Life
in the Country
or How to Keep on Keepin' On

Nick: Almost everybody who moves from the city to a rural existence has a "worst" day of their life. It is sometimes triggered by an accumulation of small mishaps and minor dissatisfactions, but that doesn't make it any less personally devastating: the cow keels over; little Fifi is chowed down by coyotes; the garden's expected harvest goes instead to blister beetles, squash bugs and slugs; a skunk takes up residence under your kitchen.

Anita: One acquaintance, another city-to-country-transplant, shakes her head when she recounts her worst experience: awakening her first day at their new rural home, looking out the kitchen window — expecting, perhaps, Bambi — and seeing (horrors!) great, dark, *swarming* creatures *everywhere*. They were as big as cocker spaniels, gray and coarse, with large eager front teeth, milling and digging around her new rosebushes, popping up from somewhere deep underground... some kind of hideous subterranean monsters. She said, "I just stood there and screamed and screamed."

Turned out to be groundhogs.

Bigfoot.
(Photo credit: Justin Evangelista)

Country life is full of variables. No nine-to-five certainties here. Sadly, this culmination of events, this special day of awfulness, is often the crossroads of a family's continued participation in the back-to-the-land dream. It is the metaphorical brick wall folks who toss predictability to the wind ultimately chance colliding with.

These less than wonderful experiences then become a test of resolve and purpose.

Nick: My day came seven months, fifteen days, and a handful of crumpled hours after our arrival at our farm from Los Angeles.

The lead up to this, of course, was sad.

It was winter.

Chapter Four
The Worst Day of Your Life in the Country
or How to Keep on Keepin' On

43

It was really, really, really cold.

Anita and I were unprepared for real weather. Whoever wrote the Christmas tune *Walking in a Winter Wonderland* never had to do any serious **living** in a winter wonderland, I'm sure of that.

Pond in winter — not too cold for geese.
(Photo credit: Justin Evangelista)

From replacing terminally shattered water pipes (when I had to go under the house and lie in icy mud) to unsticking frozen parking brakes on our car (when I threw my back out) to herding sheep off a hillside in thirty below zero weather (when my eyelids kept freezing shut) we had our hands and our brains full. We refer to this time — our first Ozark winter — fondly as "The Black Hole."

44

Remember, in Southern California, "winter" means putting on a heavy T-shirt — where the seasons consist of summer and not-quite-summer. Where "sawing logs" — an eternal country pastime designed to provide wood for the heating stove — only means taking a nap in the warm, lazy sun.

The freezing blast that came sweeping down out of the North, and grabbed hold of us by our nerve endings, was neither expected nor appreciated. No matter how hot we cranked up our wood stove in the living room, we froze if we weren't standing within two feet of the blaze. Needless to say, not very much got done around the farm.

Physically, it was tough, but psychologically, it was a killer. I remember our first Christmas on the farm more like a funeral, conducted in a perpetual deep freeze. Ho, ho, ho! It was very easy to forget why we moved to Missouri.

For a long time, Anita and I alternated being depressed; her one day, me the next, and so on down the line. I don't know what would have happened if we'd ever been depressed on the same day together, but I bet it would have made the headlines of our local newspaper.

�;�;�;�;�;�;

In the beginning, we didn't think our life could get any worse than it was.

But it often did.

Each new low point, thought to be the lowest we could sink, only proved to be the prelude to some new, even more dismal event. But diligence and perseverance are sometimes rewarded. One day, we managed to locate the absolute rock bottom of our life.

As one might expect, this day began poorly.

Around 9:00 a.m., we ran out of firewood for our stove. Then, it started to snow.

Chapter Four
The Worst Day of Your Life in the Country
or How to Keep on Keepin' On
45

At least we still had food. Some canned tuna, some puffed rice cereal, and some corn meal. Oh yes, we also had some goat milk. A couple of late paychecks for published magazine articles had reduced us to poverty rations. Hey, we were ready for anything — short of reality.

My job for the day was set: find firewood. Period. This was not the sort of balmy, blissful, carefree country existence I'd imagined for myself when I was still living in the city.

I bundled up before heading out to the woods. Anita made sure of that. A couple coats, a sweater, long johns, heavy pants, a long scarf, thick gloves, a hat pulled down over my ears, and snow boots. It's a wonder I could move, much less gather wood.

I looked outside at the lead-gray sky. The snow was really coming down. It had already spread a thick white mask across the countryside, turning the familiar into something distant and alien.

"If you start to get too cold, come back in the house right away," Anita warned me.

I frowned. "You never let me have any fun."

"Listen to me. People get hypothermia real easy in weather like this. Then, you know what happens? They die."

"Well, it's a change of pace."

"Not much."

I grabbed up my handsaw, and threw open the front door. "Why, exactly, did we move here? I can't remember."

"Just be careful," she said.

"You bet."

The woods were silent except for the soft, hissing whisper of snow sifting down through naked tree branches.

I began looking for suitable wood for our stove. Which was no simple task. Almost everything on the ground was buried in snow.

Country Living is Risky Business

46

Of course, when I did find a log worth cutting up, it was pretty much frozen solid. Which made sawing nearly impossible. But I had to keep at it. We had to have wood to burn if we wanted to stay warm. There wasn't any way around it.

Laboring in cold weather, I found, is very tiring. I had to stop every few minutes and rest. It wasn't long before my arms were ready to drop off.

After about an hour's work, I had a pile of cut wood that could best be described as a joke. Besides being almost too damp to burn, it would have been used up in less time than it took to gather it.

It was discouraging.

I was attacking a fallen tree branch, a piece of wood maybe ten inches thick, and making almost no headway at all, when something clicked in my brain and I just gave up.

Dropping my saw on to the ground, I sank heavily on to a rock. I buried my face in my folded arms.

"I'm finished," I groaned. "I can't do this anymore. I'm just going to stay here until the snow covers me up."

A novel I'd read in high school, *Giants in the Earth*, came to mind. It was about nineteenth century Swedish immigrants in Minnesota. I think it was Minnesota. Anyway, at the end of the story, the hero went out into a blizzard to find a doctor for his sick friend. They found the hero the following spring thawing out up against a haystack. A happy ending. That's how I saw myself presently finishing up my stint on earth.

I sat there, listening to the gentle woosh of the falling snow. I could feel little mounds of icy stuff building up on my shoulders and the back of my neck.

Then, oddly, I started to get bored. This freezing to death stuff took too darned long. I raised my head wearily.

So much for suicide. I rose stiffly to my feet and brushed the snow off my head. Gritting my teeth, I picked up my saw.

Chapter Four
The Worst Day of Your Life in the Country
or How to Keep on Keepin' On
47

By the time I'd finished sawing — four hours later — I'd gathered over two hundred pounds of wood. This seemed like a good collection. It was enough to last us for a day or so, once the moisture evaporated. I was about ready to collapse, but my task was far from over. The next step: carry the logs home. It took five trips to get all the wood on to our front porch, where it could dry out. Along the way, I found slippery patches in the snow. I fell down a bunch of times. They were good, hard, painful falls, too. Real "legs up in the air" splats, with wood landing on top of me.

Physically, I felt the kind of total, awful, overwhelming exhaustion you can only feel when you realize your best effort isn't going to be enough. But I completed my job.

I didn't leave behind one piece of wood, either.

It was nearly dark out, around 5:00 in the evening, when I came staggering through the kitchen door and threw myself down in a chair.

A least it was warm in the house. And it was so bright.

"All done?" Anita asked.

I nodded.

"How's the wood burning?" I asked.

"It was a little slow to get going," Anita said, "because it was so wet. But now it's fine."

"Well, that's something." I looked up.

"By the way, what's for dinner?"

"A real treat," Anita said.

"What?"

"Corn meal soup."

I blinked. "What?"

"Corn meal soup. Corn meal, water, salt, heat. Corn meal soup."

"Corn meal soup?"

"That's what we have. I would have made corn bread, but we're out of oil. And eggs. And flour. I put some tuna in it to give us something to chew on." My wife paused. "It's better than starving."

"I hate it when you quote Plato." I closed my eyes. I could feel trauma setting in.

Anita put her head on my shoulder. "It'll be okay."

I ate my corn meal soup. I ate three full bowls of it (I was hungry; I'd have eaten a cooked rat if we had one). But to this day I can't think of corn meal soup without becoming morbidly depressed.

I fell asleep right after dinner, and stayed asleep until the following morning.

✖✖✖✖✖✖

The very next day, the long-awaited checks arrived in the mail.

The weather warmed up, and the snow started to melt. First thing, we acquired a cord of wood. Nice, dry, ready-to-split stuff.

Then, we went to town and bought lots of food.

We even paid some bills.

Things just *had* to get better now.

They did.

It only took another nine winters of practice.

✖✖✖✖✖✖

There is one primary strategy for surviving the inevitable bad spell: *marching doggedly on.* That's it. You get up and go through the motions.

You might hate what you're doing, hate where you are, try to figure out how you can go back to the safe and familiar and

Chapter Four
The Worst Day of Your Life in the Country
or How to Keep on Keepin' On
49

predictable life you once knew (but realize you can't), and you just go on.

At some point, it doesn't hurt so much any more.

Then, the situation starts to improve.

Pretty basic strategy, huh?

Thing is, it always works.

Chapter Five
Making a Fire:
I am the Match Stick

Think about this one: One of the big traumas we encountered when we moved to the country was learning to use the wood-heating stove in our living room. When we bought our farm, and saw that it had a woodstove already in the house, we were overjoyed. It was part of our rural dream to heat ourselves with fires we made ourselves. How rustic! How back-to-the-land! We thought this, of course, with the ignorant bliss that accompanies fantasy and lack of experience.

You can imagine our surprise when reality set in.

Ignorance

Coming into our first winter in the Ozarks, we had never once in our lives made a fire before, not even when camping (which we never did, anyway). When we were growing up, we lived in houses that had natural gas heat. This was in Southern California, the land of summer and not-quite-summer.

If it got down to fifty degrees, now that was winter. Of course, if you had an older house, you might have a fireplace fueled by gas. Want a fire with a (fake) log or two? Turn on the gas. That's living!

This year's firewood, step one!
(Photo credit: Justin Evangelista)

We remember looking into our wood-heating stove for the first time, stunned into silent disbelief. It was empty. No fake logs. Just a heavy metal grate. Hey, how do you make this thing *go?* Suddenly things were as complicated as trying to put together a bike for your kid on Christmas Eve.

Okay, there's this space inside your stove, and you somehow are supposed to take some logs or wood, and create warmth. Hmmmmm!

The Stove

Think about this: a wood-heating stove is just a place to hold a fire so it doesn't burn your house down. It can be more "efficient" than an open fireplace, simply because the rate of burn is controllable (by opening and closing air vents), and you can slow the movement of heat up your chimney (by way of a "damper"). The more heat your stove can retain after it's warmed up, the better it will radiate heat to you and the rest of the house when the fire has died down. This means: heavier (cast iron vs. sheet metal, for instance) is better.

You just don't hold a match to a log and it bursts magically into flame. Wish it was true, but thermogenesis (heat-making, to you) only works that way in the movies. Or if you happen to be one of those spontaneous combustion people.

So, what do you do?

Research

First, do some reading. There are a number of country living books out there that have a chapter covering the topic (we'll tell you momentarily how we solved the fire starting problem), and you can decide what will work the easiest for you. Remember, easiest is the key word here. You don't want to be messing around for an hour with starting a fire early some winter morning when it's ten below zero outside. Easy translates into consistent, which translates into warm.

And here's something else: you have to understand that the stove has to absorb heat from the fire before it will start radiating heat. On a really cold morning, when you're in your living room and that stove metal is icy cold and you can see your breath in front of you, this can seem like it takes forever. So, know what you want to do, and be consistent. From our own experience, trying to cut corners on whatever process you use, just because you're cold and impatient, only prolongs your condition.

I am also the woodsman.
(Photo credit: Justin Evangelista)

Our Method

Okay, we tried lots of ways to start fires in our stove, but nothing seemed to work. Sometimes, we think, the experts forgot to mention the subtleties of what's happening inside the big metal box... it's so obvious to them, you know. This can leave you scratching your head, and maybe using your book for fire starter.

Certainly, each stove you encounter seems to have its own personality, and because of this, sometimes you must do some tinkering with your recipe. One man's sure-fire method may be your passport to frustration.

Anyway, none of the standards worked for us. We decided to experiment until we found something that worked on a consistent basis. Here's what we have finally settled on:

1. Take an empty feedbag/dog food bag (newspaper burns too quickly), roll it up loosely, and place it in your stove's fire compartment.
2. Light the bag on fire.
3. At the same time, start putting kindling on top of the feedbag. Kindling can consist of dry twigs, small pieces of dry old lumber, and old pieces of bark. Pine and a little bit of cedar wood are fast-and-hot-burning starters. Torn up cardboard boxes also will start a blaze.
4. Once the kindling is burning well, you can now put small pieces of split wood onto the fire. Lay them split-side down to the flame. Remember that "fire burns 'up'," so put new stuff on top of already burning wood, leaving room for air to circulate around the flames.
5. Finally, with the small pieces aflame, you can set a big piece of wood or two onto the fire, and it shouldn't go out when you shut the stove door. If it does go out, find another feedbag and start over.
6. Finally, be diligent. You can't go away, and just forget about the fire, thinking you're set for a few hours. It will burn out, and you will have to start all over again. It's best to get into a habit of checking the flames every fifteen or twenty minutes, until you can pretty well gauge the rate your wood burns.

    When you'll be away for a while, or for overnight "fire holding," turn the air intake down low enough to just keep the coals alight. Later, when you open the intake, the fire will spring back to life.
7. If you do this right, you can light a fire in the fall, and put it out in the spring — the famous "one-match-fire." Of course, we haven't quite figured this one out yet — but we

have had three-match winters. At that rate, our stored match supplies should last sometime into 2370.

General Advice

1. Make sure you have a damper (an adjustable metal plate usually situated somewhere in your stove pipe). Without one, all the heat you produce will just go up your chimney. Experiment with positions of the damper: fully open, half open, almost closed. When the wind is coming from specific directions, you may find it easier to start fully open, or mostly closed. Although you can't completely close a damper (small amounts of air continue to leak through), you also don't want to! That would force smoke and combustion products into your home — bad, very bad. If your fire gets a bit too hot, you can close the damper about half or three-quarters to slow it down — at the same time closing the air intakes near the front of the stove.

2. Don't use leaves — dry or wet — to get your fires started (we tried this in a moment of desperation). Of course, if you're into sending really thick and smelly smoke signals, by all means give this method a try.

3. Watch out for backpuffing (that's smoke coming back down the chimney into your stove and into your house). This can come from a badly placed chimney or stovepipe in relationship to the air flow around your house. You can get special caps to put on your chimney/stovepipe to combat this. We used to have a saying in our house: "Wind from the south, smoke in your mouth," because the external stovepipe for our wood-cookstove was in a position to catch and drive all those great southern winds right down into the house. Get yourself a backpuffing cap

if you find yourself in this situation. Smoke does nothing for the interior of your house, believe us.

4. Clean your chimney and stovepipes at least once a year — twice is better — to prevent creosote building up. Creosote is a black, gritty, oily byproduct of burning wood that clings to the inside of every chimney set-up. But you don't have to know what it is exactly; you just don't want it around. It can ignite and generate a flue fire that will hit temperatures of up to 2000 degrees. It can heat surrounding walls to ignition temperatures, and torch your entire house. Besides, you don't want Santa Claus to get too dirty when he slides down your chimney, do you?

If you have a brick chimney arrangement, check periodically on the inside smoke path for cracks (a mirror and a flashlight can help you with this). If you find any cracks, don't use that chimney until you get them fixed — otherwise, you risk burning your house down.

5. Don't leave anything on your stovetop that will burn or melt. Stoves get hot. They're supposed to. Also, it's not a good idea to leave clothing hanging above your stove either — stuff can fall onto a hot surface and *poof!*

In the olden days, stove burns to children were relatively common... many elderly people can show scars on hands, arms, chest, and face that they acquired as little ones — leaning or pushed against the heating stove. If you have children, make provisions for them to be kept arms-length from the stove — there are metal "stove fences" that provide an attractive and safe protection-zone around the stove.

6. If you don't have to worry about backpuffing, at least have a spark arrester cap on your chimney top. You can be sure, then, that you won't set your roof on fire. Also, the cap will keep birds from flying down your chimney.

7. Remember to empty your stove's ash pan often. A build-up of ash cuts down on air flow. Fire needs air to stay alive. Place the ash in a *metal* ash scooper — even if it is cold and looks completely out. Put the ash outdoors where there are no flammables nearby. Spread it over your garden area when it is damp or snowy outside. Every fall, somebody will make it into the local paper — for storing ash in paper sacks, leaving it on a porch or wood floor, or for pouring "dead" ash on crisp, dry, tinder. Try to avoid this kind of notoriety.

8. Make sure that the wood you burn has been aged for a while — a few weeks at least. Six months is better. A year is ideal. Wood cut from a live tree (green wood) is full of moisture, and will not burn at its best. Burning green wood also causes creosote.

9. Do not burn treated wood in your stove. The chemicals in the wood create poisonous smoke. And smell really nasty. Ask us how we know.

10. Very large pieces of wood should be split. They will burn better that way.

11. Soft woods like pine and poplar burn hot and fast, but they don't last. Hard woods like oak and hickory burn more slowly, and give off a steady heat.

12. Do not use slick magazine pages to get your fire going. They just smolder and clog up the air flow around your wood.

13. Keep a supply of firewood on your front porch or under a roof or tarp, out of the snow and rain. Guess what? Wet wood is hard to catch on fire, and it burns badly when it does.

14. Repeating for emphasis: Watch where you dump the ashes from your ash pan. Often they have red hot embers hiding in there somewhere, and you can end up setting your yard

on fire. Of all the fires you make, that will be the easiest one.

15. Needless to say (but we will anyway), you can't make lasting fires without wood to put in your stove. This means that running out of said wood is a bad thing. Some old timers suggest that you always have two years of firewood in reserve; but at least be ready with a couple months worth of seasoned wood (this means dried as opposed to salt and peppered) on hand.

    And, if you have to cut your own wood, get yourself a chain saw. They make a lot of noise, and there's a certain amount of risk involved, but if you are careful and don't get arrogant, you will not get hurt. Handsaws may be traditional and woodsy, but they make wood collecting a life's task. Be efficient. Also, since, you'll need to split some of the wood you cut, you'll need a good ax or maul. Don't be cheap when you buy one: a good wood splitting tool is worth its weight in gold. It's a fact: no wood, no fire.

16. Okay, now here's a really important thought (we've saved the best for last), don't try to start your stove fire with gasoline, lighter fluid, butane, barbecue starter, or diesel fuel just to get it done fast.

    People do it, but this is crazy.

    The fumes from these liquids are explosive. If you decide to use this method for starting fire, someday you will burn up yourself, your house, or both. On the bright side, you'll finally have a story written about you in the local newspaper. We know someone who uses diesel fuel to start his stove fires, liberally splashing it on his pants and floor at the same time. He won't listen to reason. It's scary.

    Remember this: Ultimately, you, yourself, are your best fire making tool. Your thoughts and actions will always influence the outcome of whatever process you choose to follow. Order and reason are your best bets. Haste, frustration, and random acts are your enemies. It's your choice.

You are the match stick.

Chapter Six
Some Thoughts on
Home Preparedness

Most of the urban world lives on the brink of running out. Often only the intervention of last minute measures saves us from this possibility becoming a reality. And we never notice this because the supermarket is just down the road, and it has everything we need right there.

Right?

You need a new mindset out in the country. Having a well-stocked pantry and medicine shelf is not a fond dream for the future but the necessity of now.

Why?

Because there will be times, living out in the country, when you won't be able to get out, and you will need to have enough food and stuff put by to see you through this time. It may last a day; it may last two weeks; it may last a month. We're not talking about apocalyptic societal breakdowns or the Road Warrior world. We're talking about weather problems, your own transportation and home system breakdowns, electrical power interruptions, medical emergencies, and the occasional job layoff — fun stuff! The question, once you are outside the city, is not if, but when one of these might attach itself to you.

This is a fact.

62

The Mindset

You can't live day-to-day in a life that has these demands and realities as part of its makeup. You will hit the brick wall, and it will hurt. Believe us. We tried it, and have the battle wounds from reality to prove it. It is best to develop the mindset that recognizes such eventualities and prepares for them. In such situations, it is always best to be over-prepared than to find you don't have enough to make it through your emergency. Remember the Titanic? Just a few more lifeboats, a simple thing, and the disaster wouldn't have been so tragic.

Systems

So, how do you begin with home preparation?

First, examine the various systems around you, see how they work, and try to arrange for some kind of backup. This is vital. Especially, examine the systems that provide your personal "infrastructure:" home, water, food, warmth and cooling, transportation, medical needs, emotional and spiritual support. If the pegs are knocked out from under one of these, you can find yourself floundering in no time.

We can't tell you specifically what to get or how to do it — because every family situation will be slightly different according to the location, wants, and needs of each person who reads this — but most of what we've written explains how we *didn't* handle this well. And how wickedly unpleasant our subsequent education has been.

Food

Having plenty of food, of course, is a good place to start when planning out your preparedness. Everybody eats. But what should you stock up on? A lot of people will suggest "survival" food, because it has a long shelf live (up to twenty years in some cases). But here's the way it really is: buy foods you like and will readily eat, foods you enjoy. Some survival food is, at best, digestible. If you can tolerate them, by all means, go for it. But the last thing you need during a disaster is a food mutiny from your family.

Also, survival food is expensive. If you feel the only way to build up a pantry is with the big bucks for super-duper nitro-packed gourmet menus, you'll never get it done. Every town has a discount food mart where you can get cases of vegetables and the like at a big discount. Do this. And, again, buy what you like to eat. If canned spinach reminds you of the contents of your nose, don't buy it, no matter how nutritious it might be for you. You won't eat it. Buy canned peaches and tomatoes and corn and carrots and peas. They're cheap, filling, and nutritious — you can hide them in casseroles. Buy candy bars: they may not be big on vitamin content, but they can give you a boost of energy when you need it.

Think about this, and start collecting food. You may also want to look into doing some canning on your own. There are dozens of books available free at your local library, or for low cost from the extension office, and even over the Internet. This is a useful skill, not hard to learn, and can save money in the long run. Plus, it's fun.

If you've got children, that "nature hike" through the hills can provide you with the means for a good lesson in local ecology and "wild-food" supplies. Field-guide books to edible wild plants of your area will help you identify the goodies — try to collect enough for a full and tasty meal, and you'll understand why our ancestors developed stable agriculture.

64

Energy

Your power will go off. We guarantee it.

Have flashlights, battery chargers, rechargeable batteries, candles, oil-lamps, and, if you can afford it, maybe a generator. (Buy a good one — diesel, with an 1800 rpm engine. Having a cheap one you can't rely on is as good as not having one at all.)

Tools

The tools you'll need will definitely depend on what you are doing with your life in the country. Buy a number of shovels, hammers, pliers, saws, wrenches, screw drivers (flathead and Phillips), a sturdy staple gun with lots of staples of different sizes, and two pairs of wire cutters (you always manage to lose one pair outside) will always be needed. Also, boxes of various kinds of nails, screws, bolts, and nuts will definitely come in handy.

Have extras of anything you use routinely.

Health Care

Stock up on disinfectants for those sure-to-happen cuts and gashes. Rubbing alcohol is a must. So is hydrogen peroxide. And a good antibiotic ointment. Have bandages of various sizes, sterile gauze pads, and medical tape. Take a good first-aid course. Even if you despise vaccinations and the AMA, be sure everybody in the household gets a tetanus vaccination, and keep them up-to-date. Tetanus is a bad way to die, and easy to prevent with these shots.

Stock up on vitamins, the pain killers you can buy over the counter, pink bismuth stuff for stomach problems, antidiarrhea pills, antacids, cough drops, and fever-reducers. Toothpaste, shampoo, and soap should be on this list, too. Buy when these come on sale, and you will never run out! There are "tooth repair kits" for those emergencies when a filling comes loose, and ointment painkillers for the waiting period before you see the dentist. Herbal remedies for toothaches, such as clove oil, work just fine, too. Neighbors who are nurses, paramedics, and first responders can often provide good advice — just remember that this shouldn't be considered a "free good;" bring along some of that homegrown meat or a home-canned jam to share.

Plant an herbal garden — garlic, rosemary, dill, comfrey, chamomile, sage and more exotic items — these all provide nutrition as well as health-care assets.

Livestock and Pets

And make sure you don't forget to provide for the animals in your care, in case you are thrown off track. They need to eat, too. Having extra dog food, cat food, and the like is a good idea. All pets need a rabies shot — for your safety and for theirs!

A surplus of hay and grain for your goats, sheep, horses, pigs, whatever, will only lessen your worries when a lack of money or weather interrupts your normal flow of supplies. We try to keep at least "one season" ahead, so that we could run without outside inputs for several months... if we had to.

The Question Mark

What else will you need in your quest for preparedness in the country? We can't answer this for you. Awareness of your systems ends up being your own responsibility. A good idea for one person might be totally extraneous for another. In the end, you must come to these realizations on your own.

Remember, preparedness is as much a mindset, a way of viewing your world, as it is a physical act. If you do not see what needs to be accomplished, you will not do what needs to be accomplished.

Chapter Seven
Thinking in the Long Term

The Home Orchard

One morning, you'll wake up, and the stark realization will hit: *this is for real... we're really here... we're **stuck** here, at least for now... this is the rest of my life that I'm looking at.*

If this doesn't give you the shakes, you're not thinking right yet.

When you realize — fully understand down to your tootsies — that *what you do with your homestead **right now*** is going to make or break your success for the rest of your time on earth (and maybe affect your family's continued existence), the shock of that realization can be an excellent motivator.

What will you be doing twenty years from now?

If you make the right plans **and** carry them out, you can be out of debt, own your home and lands, have soil and fields that are vastly improved over your current surroundings, have so much nutritious food continuously on hand that you can sell some to other people, have the means and skills to keep warm in winter and cool in summer, plus have a wealth of practical abilities of self-reliance **and** the self-confidence that goes along with them.

Or, if you don't make plans, make the wrong ones, or don't carry out the right ones — you could be sitting in that muffled gray cubicle, glugging bitter coffee, worrying that you'll be the next wage-slave downsized, and wondering where your own "good old days" went.

Well, okay. Maybe it's not that simple. It's *never* that simple. But you get the idea — *you've gotta have a plan.*

One Piece of the Plan

This book can help you think your way through your options, but we want to place special emphasis on one aspect of your homestead's future: the home orchard. Both of us have always lived where trees provided at least a little food for home use.

Nick: I grew up in Burbank, California — we had a huge old lemon tree, that always seemed to be in bloom and covered with bright yellow fruit at the same time. There was never a need to buy a lemon, and I still have resistance to paying for one now! Neighbors had citrus of various kinds: orange, grapefruit, and still more lemons, and I remember they always wanted to give us fruit, and we couldn't use up what we had. One neighbor had a plum tree. As kids, we'd climb that tree and feast on those ripe, juicy, purple plums, bombing the pits on passersby like we were crazed wild monkeys!

Anita: We lived in two houses on the same street in Los Angeles at different times. One had two large old avocado trees in the yard, and an apricot tree over a patio — one of my earliest memories is of sitting on the rough branches of an avocado tree and munching one of the rich, green fruits right down to the seed. The other house, an old one for the area, had apricots, peaches, a giant old Metheley plum, Thompson seedless grape vines, and a lemon tree. The neighbors, a pair of old maiden ladies, had Queen Anne yellow cherries, figs, and even a pecan tree! I love apricots, but can't stand to buy the awful tasteless hard *things* that pass for apricots in the supermarket... so I haven't eaten one in over 18 years. Kinda pitiful.

It always seemed to us that fruits of all kinds were just naturally free... they were so plentiful and so tasty that they were *given away*, almost forced on you by their sheer numbers!

So, it came as something of a surprise that our Ozark homestead only had three fruiting trees on it when we moved in: a very old sickly yellow apple, a sour cherry, and an ancient mulberry. (Both the apple and the mulberry died within a couple years.) More surprising, still, was that few rural people planted or maintained orchards of any kind. Oh, sure, there were a couple old houses with a fruit tree or two nearby (old overgrown apples still struggle along), but the "backyard orchards" that we imagined belonged on every small farm just don't exist any longer.

Why not?

Part of the reason has to be from changes in "lifestyle:" people, by and large, aren't willing to can or preserve fruit — why bother when you can get it so cheap at the supermarket, and without all the work? Besides, who's got the time anymore with the wife working in town?

Part of the reason comes from increasing mobility: people "follow the jobs," and buy and sell homes like any other commodity — why plant a fruit tree, when you won't be there long enough to see it bear anything?

Part of the reason is oriented to "curb appeal:" fruit trees aren't as "attractive" as exotic bloomers, make a "mess" when their fruits are unused and fall to the ground, and actually require a few hours of care and pruning each year — why go through the effort, when all you want is something that looks good?

Each of these reasons is a "piece of the plan" for someone, and fits in with their understanding of their life and its imagined direction.

A Little Dose of Reality

All of this presumes that the values, social system, and lifestyles of today will be the same ones operating 20 years from now. What if... *what if... things CHANGE!!!* Imagine that truckers can't get cheap diesel, and fruits cost twice or three times as much to transport — apples might cost $1.50 each, for instance. Sound unreasonable? We find it unreasonable when a Braeburn apple costs 50 cents today at the local supercenter... twenty years ago, an apple cost 5 cents at the market — so they are a whopping ten times more expensive today! Allowing for inflation, it should only be four times more expensive, based on 1978 dollars. We don't expect supermarket fruit to get cheaper, or better tasting, anytime soon.

But a single standard apple tree in your backyard can easily give you two hundred *pounds* annually of the best-tasting fruit you ever ate starting in only seven years — a single dwarf tree can give you 50 pounds annually starting in three or four years. And both can keep doing the same thing, year after year after year — for the *rest of your life.* Maybe for the rest of your kids' lives, too, if they take care of the trees.

Planning Ahead

Even so, to get that kind of bounty, *somebody's* got to put that tree in the ground. You're a likely candidate.

First, you need to know your area — some trees can't be grown where there are hard freezes: tropical ones like citrus, avocado, banana, sapote, figs, cherimoya and so forth. Other trees *require* a period of sub-freezing weather in order to fruit — most of the supermarket fruits we're familiar with including apples, pears, peaches, nectarines, "pluots" or "apriums," plums, cherries, and so on. Garden seed catalogs, or fruit tree catalogs will indicate "zones" for each part of the country — most "frost sensitive" tropical trees do well in zones 8-10 (warmer parts of the country), and most trees that are "frost required" do better in zones 7 and below (colder parts). There are "low cold requirement" trees that can do well all over (like apricots and a few types of apples), so you'll need to study your tree catalogs for these details.

Next, you'll need to recognize your own taste preferences. If you don't eat applesauce, never have, never will, you won't need much in the way of apple trees. If you hate prunes, ditto on the plum trees. If you really and truly will not preserve fruits by some method at any time in the future, and don't want to share with neighbors and friends, you probably wouldn't want more than one of any kind of tree. (If you've never had fresh right-off-the-tree fruits, you may not realize, at this point, that fresh fruit is entirely different from the supermarket stuff. Not just a little different — but worlds apart. We want to caution you that if you've never liked the "fruits" available at markets, after you've tasted your homegrown fruit you might realize you didn't plant *enough* trees!)

Pollinators

Next, you must understand that in order to bear fruit, nearly all varieties of trees (especially apples) need to have a "pollinator." A pollinator provides an unrelated pollen donation, which is acceptable to the tree and causes the flowers to become fertilized. It is the fertilization of flowers, usually brought about by bees and other insects going about their business that causes the little buds to swell into fruit.

A pollinator is essentially a tree of the same species but of a different type — for instance, all apple trees can be easily pollinated by crabapples — but cultivars of Red Delicious apples won't pollinate other Red Delicious varieties. Fortunately, you don't need a degree in botany to understand this... fruit tree catalogs will list acceptable pollinators for everything they sell.

Successful pollination is one reason to include variety in the kinds of trees you acquire.

Tree Sizes

Fruiting trees come in five basic "sizes," which represent the maximum growth potential of the tree. These are:

Miniature: Trees can be grown in pots, and even when planted in the ground only grow 4-8 feet tall. Fruits are full-sized. All miniature trees must be firmly staked to the ground or pot. May give up to a bushel of fruit at maturity, if ground-planted, 25 pounds if grown in a pot. These trees can be planted 3-4 feet apart. Zones 5-8, but can be grown in pots in zone 4 if overwintered under shelter. Starts to produce the second year after planting.

Dwarf: Trees typically grow to a maximum of 10 feet tall. Full-sized fruit, about two bushels produced at maturity per tree. These trees consist of a "dwarfing rootstock" with a grafted top-section on it — the join is a prominent knob on the trunk. Begins to produce the second or third year after planting. Plant 10-15 feet apart. Zones 4-8 (some variations).

Semi-dwarf: The most productive type of tree, for its size. Typically grows up to 15 feet tall. Shows a graft on the stem.

Full-sized fruit in 3-5 years. Several bushels possible per tree at maturity. Plant 15-20 feet apart. Zones 4-8.

Standard: Full-sized tree, may or may not be grafted (different rootstocks grow better in some areas). Grows to 25 feet tall, bearing fruit mostly on the outer edges of the branches. Can produce 100-200 pounds, or more, at maturity. Begins fruiting 5-7 years after planting. Plant 30 feet apart. Zones 4-8.

Columnar: A relatively new release of apple, these trees are actually a single mainstem, with a few twiggy branches off the sides. Grows about 6-8 feet tall, 1-2 feet wide. Can be grown in pots. Must be staked, especially in windy areas. Produces in 2 years from planting, perhaps as much as 20 pounds at maturity. Zones 4-8.

✖✖✖✖✖✖

Some years ago, a specialist tried to calculate the best type of tree for full-time orchardists to grow — he figured the initial cost for trees versus the tree's productivity over time, and factored in labor in the form of spraying, pruning, and harvesting help.

According to that specialist's calculations, he found that investing in dwarf trees cost more initially to use up the orchard space (more trees per acre), but the earlier bearing paid for that expense; they were the easiest to harvest due to their small size... but they didn't live very long for a tree, typically fifteen or twenty years. For moderate space, the semi-dwarfs were most productive for their size, plus were more easily harvested than larger trees; they lived longer than dwarfs, too. Larger standard trees lived much longer — could go for a hundred years or more — and gave a bigger harvest over time, even though they took a few more years to reach productivity, and needed much more space.

Although columnar trees didn't exist when that specialist did his work, we suspect he'd consider them something of an oddity — more an "edible landscaping" device than something you'd put in an orchard. He also didn't consider miniature trees... but someone else did a study: miniatures were somewhat more costly to install than dwarfs, but that was because they could be planted much closer together. They were exceptionally easy to harvest. Because of the closer planting, the per-acre yield was a little better than dwarf trees would have been. However, they were brittle in high winds, and trunks broke easily (stakes cost extra, too!).

As with everything else, it seems, there are pros and cons on tree types, too. Being adventurous sorts, we've got them all; better to have a fruit tree of any type than no fruit tree!

Care and Spraying

One of the really nice things about a home orchard is that it takes so little time, per year, to keep your trees healthy. In late winter, a spraying with "dormant oil" — a basic vegetable-oil-in-water emulsion — before the buds open, will smother any overwintering insect eggs. Mulching and fertilizing (organic or chemical) just before buds open will help insure a good fruit set. Fertilizing a couple times during the growing season (last time at the end of July to prevent sudden growth spurts during the autumn) keeps the trees going. Then, a winter time pruning to shape the trees, control their size, and increase yield. These are the principal and primary care activities that a fruiting tree needs.

Unfortunately, so many varieties of fruits now exist that have special requirements, weaknesses, and needs, that a typical commercial orchardist must spend a significant amount of time spraying trees against insects and fungal pests. Spray requirements differ from area to area and from season to season — and from tree to tree!!!

Our choice in this matter has been to select trees from varieties known to be "disease resistant" — such as Freedom, Liberty, Jonafree, and Enterprise apples — and to tolerate the occasional wormy peach. Additionally, we use traps to catch and control codling moth and other undesirable critters, which keeps the bug-damage to a minimum without spraying a lot of poison around. We've had some significant problems with brown-rot on peaches in the past couple wet years, so we've just begun a "spray program" using a copper-based soap solution to control the rot problem — this consists of three sprayings around the time of bud opening. That has upped our "orchard care" time from about 3 hours a year to roughly 15 hours annually.

One other thing we do that is considered loony-fringe stuff is to spray the trees several times during the season with a solution of plain water and 3% hydrogen peroxide — about 3 tablespoons of drug-store peroxide to a quart of water (one pint peroxide per gallon of water). Several years ago, we heard anecdotal accounts of improved yields on trees and garden plants sprayed with the harmless peroxide solution, and decided to give it a try. We changed nothing else in our routines (which are pretty nonchalant, anyway), but sprayed the trees at flower-bud opening — a single spraying.

The results: the old sour cherry tree that hadn't given us more than a handful of fruit annually for over eight years — gave us over 100 pounds. Peach trees that had never successfully produced a crop gave us enough to eat fresh and can that we were still making pies and cobblers the following spring. The vegetable garden produced over twice as much as in previous years — and the plants were bigger and healthier, too. We "tested" this on a small scale, by spraying one forsythia bush, and leaving another one beside it alone — the one that was sprayed flowered intensely with thousands of large golden buds and the flowers lasted longer, compared with the unsprayed one that had exactly 15 pale yellow flowers on it.

This, of course, proves nothing whatsoever in a technical sense, and doesn't explain any mechanism by which the peroxide spray might work. But it was convincing enough for us to keep using the peroxide spray routine. It's cheap, too.

The one key point in the peroxide spray routine is that it must be done after the sun sets — in the dark. Perhaps there is some change in the plant's respiration in the dark that allows the increased oxygen content in the peroxide to assist the plant in some way. But whatever is taking place in the plants, you most certainly will earn the "neighborhood wacko" award when you insist on wandering around and spraying your trees in the dark!

Ripening and Harvest

If you plan your tree selections wisely, you can actually harvest some type of fruit from late May (sour cherries) to November (Granny Smith apples). With only a few trees and a desire to mostly consume your goodies while fresh, this is certainly the best way to do it.

However, if you plan to preserve a good portion of your harvest for winter use (and don't have large refrigeration capacity for bushels and bushels of fruit), you may prefer to have your fruits all arrive at one time — so the person who does the canning at your home can get their pain out of the way all at once.

Tree catalogs show "ripening" times, the typical month when fruit will be ready for picking. Keep in mind that very early ripening fruit will also tend to bloom earlier, too — and can be nipped by late frosts. If you mix your early and late blooming varieties, you'll be assured that you get a harvest of *something,* no matter how strange the spring weather gets.

We have only one primary hint for harvesting fruits: don't bang the fruit around in the process. Dinged and damaged fruit starts the "bad apple" problem, and can cost you an entire barrelful. Handle each fruit lightly but firmly, place them (not dump or toss) into containers that are only a few fruit deep to prevent mashing or damaging the ones on the bottom, and store in a cool place, from day one.

Windfall fruit can go to your animals, and should be cleaned up before autumn sets in, to prevent spread of tree diseases.

Prices

Typically, fruit trees from *tree-grower* catalogs will run anywhere from $10 to $25 each... the lower price is seen in their "overstock" sales. In our experience, these tend to be better-quality trees than the kind available at chain how-to stores (where the guy who picks out the varieties majored in business, not horticulture). Chain store trees tend to be less expensive, though, averaging $12-$16 each. General gardening catalogs also offer fruit trees, and while the prices are moderate at $10-$16, the quality is only moderate, too.

Local nurseries, if they grow their own trees, can be an excellent source. You can look at prospective trees before you buy them, select whichever tree you want, and have it dug as you watch, in some places. Prices in our area average $10-$20 per tree. If the local nursery doesn't grow their own trees — they have them shipped in from somewhere else — you might as well shop from a catalog, just like they do.

We have been most pleased, overall, dealing with commercial orchard-supply companies. The prices on individual trees can be as low as $3-$8 each, and the quality is excellent —

just as someone who makes their living from fruit trees would expect. However, in order to get these deals, you need to shop like a commercial orchardist... which means buying a minimum of 10 trees of any given variety, or by paying $1 or so per tree extra as a "breaking charge" for splitting up a bundle of 10. When we put in our acre-size orchard, we were happy to pay the extra $1 penalty for such top notch trees — and they still cost less than $10 each, including shipping, by the time we were done. Before then, though, we usually tried to acquire one or two new trees every year... putting in a home-orchard on a budget works just as well as buying everything *en masse*.

In terms of supplies to keep your orchard going, you'll also need a spade or posthole digger to plant the trees with (make the holes larger than the root system); a portable sprayer ($20 to $300 — we use a $60 Sears model with wheels); a pruning clipper for small branches; a pruning saw for larger branches; a ladder for harvesting and pruning up high; and cardboard boxes (from the supermarket dumpster) to transport and hold fruit. And canning jars/equipment or a good-sized evaporator/drier for preserving fruits.

Final Thoughts

When we think of orchards, we frequently only think of the more familiar fruits we've already mentioned. There is an entire *world* of other types of edibles that we're less familiar with — things like small chewy sweet fruits called "Japanese raisins," and the pulpy soft cinnamon-apple-flavored "Medlars"... and even trees such as Carpathian walnuts, almonds, pecans, hickories, butternuts, filberts, and "heartnuts," with their protein, oil, incredible flavor, and beautiful hardwoods, all in one!

With a little bit of ingenuity, even those of us in the snow regions can grow "tropical" fruits like oranges, lemons, grapefruit, tangerines, limes, coffee trees, and bananas — indoors, in pots. Just plan on moving these outdoors to sunny locations during the warm months.

There's no law that says you must limit your orchard to any particular kind of fruit — so why not experiment? And, while you're at it, plan to plant a few seeds from your fruit each year... could be *very* interesting... and definitely the cheapest way to get new trees!

Chapter Eight
This Year's Goal:
Ready for *Anything*

Anita: We awakened one recent spring morning to discover a flat on the rear passenger-side tire of our station wagon, the vehicle I had planned to drive to town for a meeting. This was cause for a certain amount of grumbling and head shaking, even though there was a kind of relief that it was neither snowing nor raining.

Nick pulled the ½-ton hydraulic jack out of the rear of the wagon, jacked the car up, and cranked the lug nuts on the wheel. When it was off, he tossed the flat into the trunk of the other car, a little 2-door passenger deal that I was waiting in.

Total time off track: 10 minutes.

After I left, Nick put the (good) spare onto the wagon. I drove the flat into a little one-man repair shop on the edge of town and dropped it off on her way to the meeting. I would pick it up on the trip back home. Total time off track: 7 minutes, most of it spent getting "up to the minute" local news reports from the shop's owner's wife.

I arrived with a mere 3 minutes to spare, since I always leave 20 minutes or more early for scheduled appointments — to allow for unforeseen slowdowns. Sometime during the meeting, my mind wandered from the subject at hand... so I dug through my purse and found the list I'd put in there earlier in the week. It was items we had used from our food storage on the weekend: cans of tuna, toilet paper, some Band-Aids, condensed mushroom soup, two pounds of egg noodles, some flour and butter.

When the meeting was over, I drove to the downtown supermarket and looked at the flier in their window — the one that showed their specials for the week. I was peeved with myself for not looking more closely at the copy the market sent out in the mail... I could have saved some time and trouble by looking at several market fliers at the same time for the weekly sales.

Well, it wasn't a total waste, since butter was on sale for 98 cents a pound — one of those "loss leaders" to get shoppers into the store. Usually, it ran around $2.29, so that would be a significant saving.

I bought 15 pounds of butter, enough to last through most of the rest of the year. By buying it on sale, I spent $14.70 and saved $19.65. I crossed butter off the shopping list, and jammed the list back down into my purse.

I stopped and picked up the repaired flat ($8), and continued home. About halfway back, the car phone beeped to life — it was our daughter. Jamie had been recalled for a job interview, and needed to take the station wagon in right away — could we meet somewhere and get the repaired "new" spare into the wagon?

We agreed to meet at a rural side road. A few minutes later, I rolled the spare into the backseat of the wagon — then I unplugged the car phone and Jamie continued on to town with the phone in the station wagon with her.

When I got home, I dumped the butter into the deep freeze. While I was arranging the cubes, I noticed that the supply of frozen vegetables was getting a little sparse-looking. I made a mental note to freeze some broccoli and peas from the garden later in the week — that would boost the supply somewhat. That would be enjoyable, too, since freezing always went a lot faster than canning the same goods. Plus, there were about four cases of canned peas still sitting in storage — enough so that I wouldn't have to can peas at all this year, if I didn't want to. I didn't want to.

Nick came in from the barn. One of the goats had a "surprise" kid during the night — we knew she was bred, but thought we had several more weeks until the "big event." Nick had gathered up the fluffy dry baby, and carried her to a corner pen that we kept set up at all times during kidding season. He put the nervous mama goat in there, too, so that the pair could get comfortable with each other for a few days, and so that the youngster could get the vital colostrum (first milk) it needed without any interruption.

While he was at it, Nick pulled a clean, covered mason jar off the shelf in the barn — one of three pint-sized containers, always there, "just in case" — and milked about a cup of colostrum from the goat into it.

I took the still-warm jar of colostrum, wrote the date and name of the milker it came from on the lid, and tucked it into the freezer alongside the butter — a little more insurance for later, in case another baby couldn't get colostrum from its mom. Then, I found a clean pint-sized jar, put a lid on it, and gave it to Nick to put in the barn.

Lack of Excitement

Yes, we know that was boring. Most days in the country — or the city, for that matter — are boring.

It could have been a lot more exciting. In earlier years, it usually was... but not in a good way. In earlier times, when we had a flat tire, the spare was usually flat, too. And the second car (when we had one) typically had its own problems and wouldn't start or couldn't be counted upon.

84

We used to carry no means of keeping in touch at a distance, and paid the price in missed appointments, rushed schedules, and nights spent shivering in the cold stalled car beside a dark country road — until we acquired a CB, and then later went to a somewhat more reliable car phone. Both have limitations caused by the hills and rough terrain, but either one is better than nothing!

Keeping track of what's in storage and in the freezer is probably the most consistently time-consuming and clearly thankless task of the day — but it is the one thing that most profoundly impacts the family if it *isn't* done: somewhere in the near future, we'd run out of a particular food. That means either an unwanted rushed trip to town along with an unexpected expense, or somebody doesn't get to eat!

The colostrum? It's full of vitamins, nutrients and special antibodies that newborn kids MUST have in order to survive and grow. Kids that don't get this first milk are that much more likely to die shortly after birth. We know this as the result of hard-earned experience, by the way. In the event that some other newborn is especially weak, or that its mother goat is unable to provide it with milk, then that frozen colostrum can be thawed and slowly warmed to provide the food the baby needs. We'll save a little in case a neighbor needs some, and for the start of next year's lambing and kidding, too — but if we have quite a bit extra, we'll thaw some around Christmas and give it to the grateful barn cats!

Observe, Plan, Replace

No, we're not extremely well organized... things continue to go wrong, go awry, and get plain messed up. The difference between now and "the early days on the farm" is that we've got *backup systems* in place, and under constant monitoring.

We don't run out of vegetables, like we used to, because we *observe* our existing supply, *plan* on how much we'll probably need, and then *replace* exactly what needs to be replaced. We don't wind up stuck with a dead flat and a dead spare, out in the wilderness when we need to be someplace else, because we *observe* the status of our spares and make sure they're in good shape, *plan* to fix the flat as soon as practically able, and then actually *replace* flats immediately if we can.

Observe, plan, replace, over and over, small scale and large. Even that newborn kid, if it's a doeling, might be a replacement for another milker — and if it's a buckling, there's a good chance it will replace some other meat in the freezer later in the year. That kid is a tiny part of an overall backup system, planned somewhere on the order of six to nine months in advance of need.

We don't know how old-time farmers came to the point where this became a "lifestyle" issue... what prompted them to begin to live like this. We do know that real oldsters put us to shame in their ability to adapt to changing circumstances. The really prepared ones could go for a year without any outside input — without having to purchase diesel for their tractors, or hay for their livestock, or food for their own use, or tires, or even electricity. Sure, they'd have to change the way they do some things — but life would still go on, and they would not be uncomfortable.

We DO know what prompted us to make backups a feature of our lives and part of our daily thought patterns: *bad things happened, and we had no recourse.* Nuthin' like makin' the same mistake, over and over again, to finally spur you to develop changes in how you live. We were real slow learners, too. Took a lot to get our attention.

86

A Plan for This Year

So, now that it has finally got our attention, we don't have much excuse for ignoring the fact that we're probably going to be living right here, the same way, for the coming year.

Changes? You bet. The garden is going to be bigger, so we can spend even less at the supermarket. We'll cull a few of the goats, and add a few sheep ewes to give us more variety in the meat department. One of the pot-bellied pig boars is going into the freezer, too. One of the ponies is probably not going to survive the year (he's awfully old), and we'll need to shop for a replacement... we'll refinish the work wagon that the ponies pull, while we're at it, using enamel paints so it will last for years and years... and plan to use the wagon more and the gas-guzzling yard-tractor less.

Looks like possible drought this year, too — so we'll contract for hay early (like, right now, at the end of winter), and make a point of putting back a year's supply, just in case. Fortunately, the wood supply for the cook stove is plenty, so we won't even have to think about that.

Now is the time for you to think about your own situation — what will you need in March, July, October, or January? How much trouble will you spare that future version of yourself?

And how much trouble will you cause — because you don't fix a problem, right now?

Section Two
Animals & Livestock

Chapter Nine
The Best Dog for Country Life

Originally published in *Backwoods Home,* May-June 2000.

When you're looking for a dog to fit into your country life, there are few other topics as liable to get you into a fistfight. People get very sensitive about their dog, its breed, or its characteristics — more so, even, than they do about their own kids. After all, your kids were just *born* — with the dog, you made a *choice.* The kind of dog you have says a lot about who you are.

All right. With the sensitive part out of the way, we can get down to business.

What kind of dog is the best for a country home? As with nearly every other rural subject, it *depends...* in this case, on five crucial factors: work or pet? size and coat? temperament? kids? costs and benefits? We'll look at these one at a time.

Work or Pet?

Contrary to popular opinion, the first decision about a country dog shouldn't be, "what breed?" — it should be what the dog's purpose will be. Either the dog will be a buddy and family pet, or it will be a working partner. Here's the difference: a pet dog fulfills your feelings and usually lives in the house. A working dog performs a valuable function and has his own house or kennel outside. A working dog can also be a pet... but a pet might have a hard time doing useful work.

Guardian at work — Newfoundland crossed with Great Pyrenees, an excellent combination.
(Photo credit: Justin Evangelista)

Noble Jack, an elderly Country Pug.
(Photo credit: Justin Evangelista)

Working breeds have been bred for generations to perform a particular task. They don't need much encouragement or training — they do their work because they love it, and because every fiber of their being requires them to do it. Typical working dog breeds include Great Pyrenees (large white livestock guardian), border collies and blue heelers (medium-sized herding dogs), Labrador retrievers (large game-retrieving dogs), or foxhounds (hunting dogs). These kinds of dogs would be expected to perform specific tasks — either around the clock like the guardians, or on-demand like the border collies and hounds.

Country dog — part Hound, part Collie,
part Dalmatian — confident and rarin' to go.
(Photo credit: Justin Evangelista)

But in a backwoods setting, other "working" dogs might also fit the bill — what function do you wish the dog to accomplish? Pulling a cart loaded with firewood (St. Bernard or Newfoundland), or pulling a sled in cold weather (Husky or

Samoyed), or aggressively barking at strangers (German Shepherd or Rottweiler), or friendly greeting of strangers (Golden Retriever), or watching the kids (Collie), or even keeping the mice down in the barn (terriers), there're breeds for every task.

Pet dogs, to us anyway, are animals whose basic skill is to pal up with people. Pets can also be adequate "bark at strangers" dogs — but since their primary orientation is to "be friends" with humans, they're not as serious about this as more aggressive guardian dogs.

Smiling and happy — Doxie and Pug mix, out in the country.
(Photo credit: Justin Evangelista)

A dog is principally a pet when its "occupation" is to hang around, play with the kids, lay near the fireplace, take walks, or be a companion. Pets can be trained to perform some duties — such as herding or guarding — but their heart won't be in it. A pet will do what you ask because it wants to *please you*, not because it wants to or has a natural inclination to do it. Pets won't be able to do any task as well as a dog that has been bred for generations for a particular job.

Breeds that make good pets include: pugs, Yorkshire terriers, cocker spaniels, Basset hounds, Lhasas, poodles, and Shelties. Pets tend to be small-to-medium sized and really require daily contact, petting, and company.

Now, after determining the dog's potential "job" —

Fritz — part Sheltie, part ???, a rough-and-tumble country kid's dog.
(Photo credit: Justin Evangelista)

Size and Coat?

Once you've narrowed down your dog choices to pet or worker, you'll want to consider the animal's full-grown size — which means looking at some factors in your surroundings, as well as the dog's future "job." If the dog will be around your children, you'll probably find a medium-sized dog ideal — big enough to tolerate the kid's hair-pulling and sitting on it, but not so big that one swipe of its tail knocks somebody down. If the dog will be expected to intimidate strangers, a bigger dog with a loud bark would be best. If the dog is just supposed to keep you company while you work at the computer — then, even a small quiet curl-up-in-your-lap could be the choice.

Along with size, the length and composition of the dog's coat needs to be considered. Dogs with beautiful thick, long coats tolerate the cold very well — but really suffer in the heat; they may need to be trimmed if they seem to be overhot. On the other hand, very short-coated dogs can't take ice, snow, or extreme winds — but cool off quickly in hot weather. If you expect to work a long-coated dog during the summer, make sure it does get that trimming — but be alert to the fact that it simply may not be able to stand the heat very well, trimmed or not. Short-coated dogs will need extra bedding and wind-protection in their doghouses during the winter months.

Size and coat considerations lead naturally into —

Temperament?

By this, we mean three factors: aggressiveness, energy level, and tolerance of stress. Aggressive dogs come in big, medium and small sizes — but if your goal is a pet for your two-year-old, aggressiveness should be at the bottom of your list of desired traits. Aggressive dogs are confident, assertive, quarrelsome, willing to fight, willing to bite when needed, and tend to be stubborn and harder to train. Unaggressive dogs "just want to get along," they like everybody, and will take a one-down position to even the youngest member of the family. Unaggressive is quite different than "shy," by the way. A "shy" dog is actually an afraid or fearful animal — and may be a snappy biter when put in a stressful situation.

With energy-level, dogs are like people: some are real balls of fire, full of pep, ready to run and play at a moment's notice (terriers fit this description); others are lackadaisical and prefer to turn into couch potatoes (Basset hounds enjoy a good snooze). If you're a ball of fire, make sure your dog is one, too — or the dog will refuse to go out in the rain with you when work needs to be done. And if you're a low-key kind of person, content to spend all your time in deep thought, a high-energy dog like a Dachshund will aggravate you with its constant demands for attention and "walkies."

Tolerance of stress is a measure of the dog's capacity to endure change, noise, confusion, and erratic schedules. This trait is as individual in dogs as it is in people — some breeds seem better able to tolerate stress, but individual dogs within breeds might or might not take it well. If you're looking at puppies, one way to determine if a dog can tolerate stress is to clap your hands suddenly. Pups that scurry to cover are more sensitive to noise, and may be more sensitive to stress than the pup that stops and looks at you to see what's going on.

Kids?

The presence of children in the household makes a major difference in the types of dogs you'd want around. When our kids were little, the only dogs we had were Lassie-type collies and collie-crossbreds. Like TV's Lassie, these dogs are bright, alert, but very tolerant and protective toward "small things." One of our old collie girls even adopted a litter of abandoned kittens, nursing and washing them as well as any cat could have, until they were old enough to find new homes.

We've been horrified to speak to people who wanted to get a "kid's dog" — but were looking at Chihuahuas. Chi's are small, all right, but they have a snappy temperament and don't tolerate a lot of childish mauling very well. Plus, a chi at 7 pounds could be squashed unintentionally by a heavy child sitting down on it.

In general, friendly, even-tempered, medium-sized, sturdy, and medium-coated dogs make the best kid-dogs — and lots of people remember that mixed-breed muttley dog that was their best-friend, so many years ago. Mutts often make excellent kid dogs.

If you're planning to keep a dog for work and not as a companion, the kids won't understand — we guarantee it. Hard working dogs, like border collies, will prefer to herd rather than playing anyway — but the kids won't understand that, either. A compromise that will satisfy all involved: working dog for the task, pet dog for the kids. The worker stays outside in its kennel when not "at work," the pet sleeps in the kids' room... probably right on their beds. The kids *will* understand this arrangement!

Costs and Benefits?

How much is a good friend worth to you? A friend who would sacrifice his life for yours, one who stays with you through good and bad, who never complains, who only wants to remain at your side no matter where you go or what you do? That's what a pet dog returns over time — all in exchange for a pound of kibble a day, and some basic veterinary care.

A working dog, however, can take the place of another human by moving livestock or guarding a portion of your land. If a working dog saves two or three sheep a year from predators, it has paid for itself. If it keeps bad guys from jumping your fence and making off with your VCR, it has bought all its own dog food for a year. If it swims out to collect your shotgunned ducks, it saves you from cold and damp, and helps you keep your eyes on the flying birds.

A purebred registerable dog of any breed, as a pup, will set you back $300-plus — much less than that, and you can be pretty sure its not from a quality line. A purebred dog that is unregisterable ("no papers") will run half or a fourth as much as a papered purebred. "No papers" may mean there's a little something "not purebred" in its ancestry — perhaps an unintentional outbreeding — but these dogs resemble pure dogs of their breed, and often have the benefit of a little outcrossing to strengthen their health and temperament.

A pup should have had its "first shots" and been dewormed when you acquire it. It will still need two more routine immunizations, and at six months it should have a rabies vaccine. After that, once-a-year boosters should prevent most communicable diseases, and twice annual dewormings will keep the internal parasites under control. If you don't mind giving your own shots, "5-way" or "6-way" vaccines run about $3 per dose. In most states, rabies vaccine needs to be administered by a vet — and typically runs $6-$12.

Adult dogs of nearly every breed can be found at animal shelters nationwide — typically, the cost will be $50-$75, and that will include license, shots and spaying or neutering.

To spay/neuter is a question that most people don't think much about — we have been convinced by our social controllers that dogs are better off being "fixed." However, somebody's got to breed dogs. It's a topic that deserves a book of its own... but a family that keeps purebred male and female dogs of the same breed, either as pets or workers, and breeds them once a year — can pay for the dog's food and then some out of the sale of pups.

If this sounds like an option for you, be especially discriminating in choosing your breeding pair — get registered unrelated dogs, from different ancestry of the same breed (ask to see the AKC pedigree before purchasing), have them carefully health-screened, learn everything you can about the breed, and plan on keeping these dogs for the long-haul. Your dogs can easily last 12-15 years, long past their reproductive potential. You might not be able to sell all the pups, and may wind up with extras to support. If this seems like too much effort, then this probably isn't an option for you.

We would also caution against prematurely spaying or neutering your dog. With a little sensibility, you can prevent unwanted breedings — and it isn't uncommon to realize you want puppies out of your dog after it is three or four years old. If the dog's already been fixed, you're out of luck.

A Caution

Many people are not conscious of it, but it's true nevertheless — people often buy a dog to fit an "image," a picture of what they think country living is like, or what they think will "look good," or a dog that builds their own self-esteem. It's hard to get past these ideas — but sorting out your reasons for having a dog can help counteract the "image" problem, and will provide you with a dog that truly fits your needs (not just your imagination).

There are fine dogs in every breed and among the world of mutts — your local library probably has an encyclopedia of breeds that describes traits and characteristics. That's a good place to start your dog-search. A few visits to the local animal shelter will also indicate what breeds and crossbreeds are typical in your area, give you an idea of "full grown" sizes for various breeds, and introduce you to some very nice people who volunteer there.

Then, you can know with confidence, what the "best" dog for your part of the country will be!

Chapter Ten
Speculating With Livestock

Once upon a time, there were unusual animals that no one had ever raised on American farms. Why, there were emus, and ostriches, and white deer, and exotic sheep, and soft fuzzy llamas, and fancy cattle with enormous horns, and little bitty piggies, and clever ferrets, and spiky miniature hedgehogs. And they were *soooo* cute and strange and uncommon that people thought they should be worth an awful lot of money.

And, for a time, they were.

That time was about 1983-1995. Llamas went from $500 per critter to over $5000. Ostriches went from a nearly worthless oddity to over $25,000 each. Ostrich eggs, *alone,* sold for $5000 each — hatching not guaranteed. Extra muscular sheep and meaty goats came in from overseas as *straws of semen* at $350 each — you provide the female animals and live birth was *not* assured. Pot-bellied pigs went from $25 for a piglet born in a pen raising lab animals, to $750 for one born in someone's garage.

Somebody made an awful lot of money.

Somebody else went broke in a very big way.

We can look at the history of the "ostrich bubble" in the U.S. for a rough guideline of how this sort of thing takes place.

Llama and friend.

Bad Times Makes for Strange Decisions

The setting: early 1980s. The cattle market is very poor — for the umpteenth year in a row. Producers who have been raising cattle on their family homesteads since Reconstruction are going broke. Environmentalists are making it desperately hard for Western ranchers to bring in an annual profit. Bankruptcies are on the rise. Cattlemen are more desperate than they have been since the last "bad times" in the 1930s.

They start looking for ways to diversify and at least break even for the year. They try marketing "extra-lean" beef for the ever-dieting consumer who thinks fat is some kind of great evil manifested on earth. They find and start breeding lean cattle like Longhorns and Brahmas... and for those producers, the money begins to trickle in.

Somebody, somewhere, remembers that when he was a kid there used to be ostrich farms — and that ostrich meat is pretty lean, too. Maybe they recalled hearing about the thriving 1920s-era Cawston Ostrich Farm in South Pasadena, California, that used to sell plumes to the film industry, giant ostrich egg omelets to tourists, and frozen ostrich meat to gourmets. Hey, somebody said, maybe that would work again — we could use the corrals and trucks we've already got, use basically the same grain (well, maybe add a little more protein content), and those rich gourmets will just eat this stuff up!!!

So, this guy told his friends about this great idea, and they made some phone calls, and located a passel of old circus ostriches. The birds were tame, settled right in, and proceeded to lay about 20 or 30 eggs each. These eggs were carefully brooded and the first serious successful hatch took place.

By now, the friends had told their friends, who told their friends, and a few hundred cattlemen and doctors and lawyers and part-time gentlemen farmers thought they just might be able to make a pretty good turnover raising ostriches and selling the meat to those wealthy gourmets. All these guys put in bids and quickly bought up the newly hatched birds, spent a lot of money and converted their cattle and horse facilities to ostrich pens, and waited for the little ones to grow up and lay more eggs.

Meanwhile, our first entrepreneurs were rubbing their hands together with fiscal delight! The few thousand they'd invested in the startup birds had already multiplied tens or hundreds of times. Surely, this was the goldmine they'd been looking for! They wanted to share this blessing with their cattle-raising buddies, so they made more phone calls, and wrote newsletters, and started magazines. Lots of people got very excited about ostriches.

More eggs were laid, more ostriches hatched, and still the money rolled in. Nobody worked very hard to find ways to sell that abundant dark breast meat on those big birds — because there was too much demand for live birds for breeding. Small details.

Pretty soon, ostrich farmers were showing up on TV programs like *Real People* and on local human-interest news shows. Amazing! Remarkable! *Finally* a way to get parity for cattle ranchers! In the 1950s, a rancher could sell a few cows, and take the proceeds out to buy a new pickup. By 1980, it took two or three trailer loads. By 1990, a dozen trailer loads or more, depending on what kind of debt those cattle were carrying. But, it only took **one ostrich** in 1987 to buy a really spiffy top-of-line shiny new pickup, complete with CD, tape deck, air conditioning, jumpseats, and salt-safe undercoating. One ostrich, or five ostrich eggs — and you had a brand new truck.

Breeders to Breeders

Somebody who had been around a while, who had perhaps studied some history, kept mumbling about "tulip bulb mania." Like all naysayers and doom-and-gloomers, they were ignored. A few troublemakers whined that ostriches were harder to raise than cattle, took more hands-on attention, and were viciously dangerous when provoked. Some problem-child even complained that nobody was actually *using* ostriches for anything — old breeders were just selling to new breeders. Hmmph.

Articles in livestock journals described the happy former cattle ranchers who were actually paying off past debts, buying back their farms from the banks, and taking on new debts to finance the expansion of their ostrich business. More and more people talked about the excellent meat that could be produced (very beefy, very lean), and the fine oil that could be extracted (lightweight, superior for cosmetics), the beautiful uses feathers could be put to (maybe we'll bring back the "boa"), and the possible uses for the thick, speckled hide (purses, belts, boots) that the ostrich could provide. And, any eggs that turned out to be infertile could be used to make really unique display pieces — painted, or varnished, or even hollowed out with various natural scenes glued to the interior — or could be made into a special-occasion meal!

Key words: *could be.*

There were many things that an ostrich *could be.* In fact, it was a very small number of animals, compared to the total that were sold, that actually made it to the processing plant. First — who knew how to butcher and prepare these animals? Special processing facilities had to be developed, butchers had to be trained, and packaging had to be found. Oil extraction from hides was an entirely new venture. Tanning those skins was different from preparing leather from cattle or goats or sheep... and everything new cost money to invent and try out. Lots of money.

But most important — why butcher an animal for 300 pounds of meat, that could otherwise bring you $25,000 by just standing around in the barnyard? At that rate, each pound of meat was worth *eighty-three dollars.* Even gourmets thought that was too expensive. After all, it just tasted like tough beef!

Tremors raced through the group of established breeders. They began to realize that although the ostrich *could be* used for all those things (and probably many other interesting things), *there was no market.* Nobody was buying ostrich meat, or feathers, or oil, or anything in enough quantity to support the high prices of breeding stock, or even the cost of keeping all those animals.

And, inevitably, the prices began to fall... and fall... and fall. Ranches foreclosed upon. Lives ruined. Marriages torn asunder. Some people managing to sell their stock at a loss but just barely keeping the farm.

Today, in our region, fertile ostrich eggs sell for $25 each. Packaged ostrich meat goes for about $6-$8 per pound — the same as prime rib of beef.

Will We Ever Learn?

The short answer: nope. Not as a group.

As individuals, we can learn a lot from the ostrich lesson.

1. *Could be* **isn't** the same as *is*.
2. If there isn't an established market for the product *right* now, there isn't any way to make money.
3. Breeders selling to other breeders is a *dead end market* — you must have *consumers,* too.
4. When an animal's cash value wildly exceeds its product value (it's worth more standing in the barnyard than as burgers), it is overpriced.
5. Livestock that increases dramatically in value because of speculation buying... will decrease just as dramatically later.

We're not knocking ostriches here, either. They are fine animals, and people who continue to raise and market them are the hardy survivors of a true speculative mania. The memory of that mania — and the resultant fortunes gained — remains with us, though. Livestock magazines still tout the "new this" and "exotic that." Just a few years ago, the meaty Boer Goat was the "new this," and followed the same general pattern as the ostrich (but never reached those bubble prices) — and now you can find Boer kids going for $25. When we see breeders selling primarily to breeders — we can be sure that by the time the animal has become widely enough distributed to make them useful livestock, their price will fall.

Every generation will see a speculative mania in some kind of animal — exotic, wild, fancy, unique. Just try not to get caught in the next one.

Chapter Eleven
Goats:
The Ruminants From Hell

There's a passage in the *Bible* about the end times that promises the sheep will go to heaven and the goats will go to hell. We realize that's a metaphor for righteous behavior and sinful behavior, but, you know, metaphors don't just occur out of nowhere.

There are some good things about goats (you could probably find at least one good thing to say about chemical waste as well). They're hardy. They can live on the worst kind of forage. Their milk is exceptional. And when they reproduce, they'll often give you more than a single baby.

On the negative side is, well, everything else.

Goats, for those who don't know, are ruminants. That means they have four stomach chambers — the largest being called the rumen — that puts food through a number of digestive stages before it is finally processed fully. This mechanism includes a lot of *cud* (the food being processed) chewing, and an equal amount of belching and regurgitating. You're not really a full-fledged owner of a ruminant until the last two functions take place right in your face at least once. Cows are also ruminants. And sheep. And antelope. And giraffes.

The very first small livestock we bought after we arrived on our farm was a goat. We picked a goat as our first real livestock purchase because they were relatively inexpensive, as farm animals go. That was foremost in our thoughts. Cheap! We certainly couldn't afford cattle or horses. Hogs were pretty cheap, too, but we'd heard too many horror tales about hog raisers being devoured by their piggy-wiggies. And we already had enough little animals to keep us busy. We'd brought plenty of chickens, rabbits, quail, and the like, from Los Angeles.

A touch of evil?
(Photo credit: Justin Evangelista)

After that, milk was certainly a consideration. We'd had goat milk before, when we lived in Los Angeles, and we liked it. Milking seemed so wholesome, so farmy.

The final factor in our decision was that goats seemed to be "easy care" creatures. At least it appeared that way to our untutored minds. You could grab them, push them around, lead them on ropes.

Right?

No problem?

Uh huh.

We had no idea what we were doing when we went to buy our first goat. We saw an ad in the local paper: "Brush goats for sale." It sounded good to us: "for sale" — just what we were looking for. Good lines? Health? Productivity? All we cared about was whether the thing was breathing.

The sale went smoothly enough. The goat was, in fact, alive. We could tell that much. Our criteria was met. Money was exchanged. We went home with one adult female and her two two-month old kids riding nervously in the back of our Volkswagen van (goats, by the way, don't care about where they relieve themselves; we found this out immediately).

We named our goat Goaty. She was a Saanen. The Saanen is a breed that originated in Switzerland, and they're noted for their high milk output. Saanens are white, nothing fancy; your basic no-frills goat.

When we got them home, we set up a comfortable space in one of the barns for our new charges. And that area has been known as the "goat barn" ever since — no matter what animals are living in it. (It was the goat barn even when we turned it temporarily into a chicken coop.)

Nick: I should say right here that, at this point, Goaty had never been milked by human hands. Needless to say, I had never milked a goat before. I had never milked anything before. A good combination if ever there was one.

So, where do you start?

You start by forcing a struggling animal on to a milking platform, trying all the while to get a milk bucket down into a spot occupied by dancing legs. The goat bucks. She kicks your hands. She steps into the bucket (which then has to be cleaned again). She leans her full weight of maybe a hundred pounds on you. You, on the other hand, have a rational mind on your side. You counter by slugging the goat in the shoulder a couple times. Then, you force her against the side of the milking stand with one arm, and try again. My first attempt at milking yielded about three tablespoons of the white stuff. I thought that was great. I proudly carried the bucket into the house to show Anita, and she thought that was great, too. I'd actually milked something. Boy, we were really cranking now.

Obviously, this level of milk production was not going to do us much good.

I worked at it, taking my time.

On the fourth day, I began with a new resolve. I was going to fill the bucket. Goaty was getting used to me. I just had to hang in there.

I began with a new confidence. My hands squeezing firmly at the goat's teats, I watched in amazement as the milk flowed quickly and easily in spurting streams into the bucket. The level rose in a bubbling froth toward the top. Finally, there it was, right at the top. I'd done it.

Then, without warning, the goat stepped in the bucket. She did it calmly and deliberately and matter-of-factly. The milk was totally ruined, bits of hay, dirt, and manure now floating in it. She also stomped repeatedly on my hand, which hurt.

At this point, I just kind of snapped.

I wrestled the goat out of the milk stand, calling her every nasty name I could think of. Then I took the fouled milk, and poured the whole mess on her head. Actually, it went all over both of us. I didn't care. (I think I must have been under a lot of stress at the time, what with our move to Missouri and all. Yes, that must have been it.)

When I was through venting my frustration, I shoved Goaty back on to the stand, and milked out what was left in her udder.

✂✂✂✂✂✂

We don't know why exactly, but from that moment on, the goat never gave us any more trouble during milking. Ever. We've heard people say that livestock will push you, to see what they can get away with, and if you back down, or let them get away with murder, well, that's it. They've got you. We don't know if that's true, perhaps reading more into goat behavior than is actually there. But it sure does seem like it a lot of the time.

We added more goats to our livestock collection in the months that followed. Another doe, Monty, and two young bucks. Some people call them nannies and billies. In a group, they're similar to a teenage gang. They'd saunter around the barn yard like they had a chip on their shoulders, like what they really wanted was a good rumble.

Separately, they were okay, but put them together, and they'd become the worst troublemakers. They'd test every inch of fence line, looking for the best escape routes. One minute they'd be out grazing in our field, the next, they'd be in the front yard stripping the bark from every fruit tree in sight. Or they'd head over to our neighbor's barn to tear into bags of grain he'd set aside for his cattle. We'd put up new wire barriers to deter their escapes, but they were like the Mongols going around the Great Wall of China. In time, they'd find some way around or through any obstacle we constructed. Their advantage was that they had nothing better to do.

We know other farmers who've had the same problems. One guy who lives down the road from us said the only way he could keep his goats in would be to build a thirty foot concrete barrier around his property, and even then he was pretty sure that when he went out to check on them, they'd be standing on top of the wall.

Houdini had nothing on goats.

Our goats were no less difficult in other areas.

Give them the choice of chomping on a nice bale of clover hay or ripping the flowers out of your garden, and they'd pick the flowers every time. If we built a feeding trough for them, they'd climb on it until it fell over. If we built a pen or cage for another animal, they'd jump on it until it collapsed. They'd find ways of breaking into the barn where we kept hay and grain, until we were forced to chain the barn doors closed. They also acted as a bad example for the sheep that we later bought, leading them off into all sorts of reprehensible adventures — everything from disappearing regularly into our neighbor's woods to stealing food from our dogs and horses.

Juvenile delinquents!

There's this one other goat problem. It has to do with buck goats. Simply put, they smell. It's actually pretty hideous. If you've never smelled a boy goat when he's pumping out his stench full strength during mating season, you just don't know what you're missing. This odor has the power to drift for hundreds of feet on its own, a creeping, unseen supernatural force, and once it gets on you, you can't wash it away, it has to wear off. Girl goats think it's wonderful. People, by and large, don't.

Our first buck goat was a stench factory of the worst sort. We named him Stinker. There was no argument on that. He was an Alpine goat, with long, curving horns, and a beard that almost hung to the ground. He closely resembled an old medieval drawing of the devil. Stinker's favorite pastime was urinating on himself, which was probably the reason for the rather overpowering smell that hung around him at all times. That was his favorite come-on for females. Goats know where it's really at when it comes to personal grooming.

Goats, pursuing a favorite pastime, stripping the bark from a tree.
(Photo credit: Justin Evangelista)

Stinker had one special quirk. He'd been kicked in the head by a horse when he was little, and this apparently gave him an inner ear disorder of some kind. Whenever he ran, he'd suddenly end up galloping sideways. Then, he'd flip over on his back, causing his great horns to dig into the ground. So, there he'd lay, helplessly, treading sky like a flipped-over crab.

Unfortunately, as Stinker grew older, he got real mean. Maybe the damage inside his head led to a personality change. He began butting everyone and everything in sight. We just couldn't trust him anymore, so we sold him to a tough old bird who didn't care about smells or personalities. He just wanted a male goat to clear brush.

We missed Stinker. For about thirty seconds.

Tough guy on a leash.
(Photo credit: Justin Evangelista)

We know of some poor souls who made the big, big mistake of turning their goat into a pet. While they were in town one day, the beast escaped from its pen, and forced its way into their house. Once inside it proceeded to, simply put, destroy. It ate pillows and chewed on furniture, it performed bodily functions anywhere it felt like, (which, apparently, was everywhere), it knocked a TV set off a table and broke it, it somehow managed to open the refrigerator, ruined a week's worth of food, and it even ate $10 in cash out of a cookie jar.

When the unfortunates returned home, they went into shock. Needless to say, their goat stopped being a pet immediately. In fact, they mentioned something about how it soon stopped being even a goat. The remark was, "You know, they never escape from those little white butcher-wrap packages."

Yes sir, when the end of the world gets here, the sheep are going to heaven and the goats are going straight to hell.

Bet on it.

Chapter Twelve
How to Buy Your First Dairy Goat

Anita: Fresh milk is one of the gentle joys of living away from the city — fresh milk, butter, buttermilk, cream, ice cream, cottage cheese, and a fancy assortment of aged cheeses. All of these delights come to us courtesy of our dairy animals, such as cows, sheep, and goats.

Goats, being the "poor man's cow," lend themselves particularly well to a small homestead. A dairy goat and her offspring can live comfortably in a 20'x 20' corral, with only a small shed for shelter from the elements. Or she can be allowed the run of the pasture or field, so she does most of her own food-collecting.

Best of all, a dairy goat's food requirements are a mere fraction of a cow's: four pounds (a flake or two) of good quality mixed hay or access to pasture, and two to three pounds of mixed grain (corn, oats, alfalfa pellets, molasses), will keep her cranking out around a gallon of milk every day for about ten months of the year. If you bought your hay and grain in the Midwest, you'd spend around forty-five cents a day to collect that gallon of milk — less if you grow your own foodstuffs, such as pumpkin or corn. Try to find that kind of bargain at the supermarket!

Okay, you're convinced. Now, how do you find that special dairy goat? Number one and most important is to **avoid** shopping at a goat auction! While many animals sold at auction are quite fine looking, you just plain don't know enough about the animal's history, milking habits, health, or care to risk buying one of these cheap wonders.

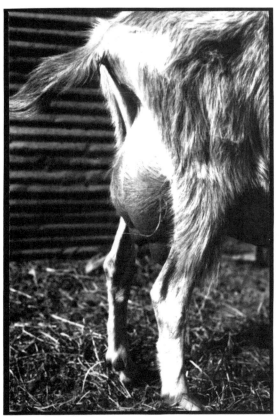

Not the best udder we've ever seen — but not the worst, either.
(Photo credit: Justin Evangelista)

Instead, check your local farm classifieds for people selling goats from their own places. This gives you an opportunity to look over the premises and see the condition of the other animals. If the place is dirty (beyond ordinary farm clutter), horribly disorganized, has sick livestock — you get the idea — get out of there! You don't need to buy into someone else's problem.

There is a mild controversy over whether the new goat-keeper should start with adult animals or goat "kids." Some folks believe that if you start with kids, you can accustom them to your farm routines and handling before they become milkers — and kids are generally cheaper than adults. Our preference, having started that way ourselves, is to buy an adult along with her kids. Here's our reasoning: the adult goat has proven that she can successfully produce offspring, she's already milking so you can take a look at the condition of her udder, and you don't have to train her to get used to milking, so there's no wait to get your first glass of milk.

Dairy Character

It's also easier to judge the animal when it is in its "finished form" — fully grown. The goat you're considering doesn't have to be purebred; it's better to start with a "grade" or crossbred goat anyway. They're cheaper — about half the price of a purebred, or less — and they're often a shade hardier, being possessed of "hybrid vigor." And you'll feel bad enough making the inevitable mistakes of goatkeeping on a crossbred animal. You can always get high-cost purebreds later.

Take a close look at your potential milker. She should show some degree of "dairy character," the outward physical traits most common in good milking animals. She should look feminine, with a narrow neck (compared to a buck or "billy's" thick heavy neck); full, evenly rounded rib cage and belly; long, flat backline; somewhat prominent hip bones; strong, straight front legs; and solidly placed feet. There's a great deal of variability here — some nannies have narrow chests, but milk fairly well, or are a little swaybacked. These are not desirable traits, and ultimately end up reducing the animal's potential milk production. But since you're not going to enter the animal in any shows (crossbreeds can't compete), it doesn't matter if she's not a perfect physical specimen. It's more important that she's healthy.

She should look well-balanced and happy; a few ribs may show very, very slightly, but she shouldn't be rail thin. Her hair coat should be clean and shiny, her eyes clear and free of matter in the corners. Depending on the breed, she may have very upright ears, pendulous long ears, or no outward ears at all. The insides of her ears should be clean. She should be free of grape-sized lumps or abscesses under her skin.

She may or may not have horns, either because the horns were removed when she was a kid or she was born without any. Some goatkeepers are adamant about removing horns, believing that goats with horns will hurt each other and damage breeding bucks. There's a certain amount of truth to this — goats butt and will use their hard sharp horns vigorously. Some does will even batter their fellow nannies' udders mercilessly. If you have woven wire fencing, a few particularly dim horned nannies will persist in poking their heads through and not be able to pull back out, necessitating a series of rescues.

However, horns are also the goat's natural protection, which they will use against marauding dogs and other predators. We've kept goats both with and without horns. The only time we had a real problem was when a doe tried to jump for the milking stand when Nick's attention was on the udder — he got bumped in the forehead by one horn, and subsequently developed a nice black eye. He told our friends that I gave it to him!

Teeth, Feet and Udder

Assuming you're looking at an adult doe (or nanny goat), there are three main features you must closely inspect before you part with your hard-earned cash: teeth, feet and udder. If the goat is lacking in any one of this "triangle" of traits, she's not worth bringing home. Ask the goat's owner to place her in a pen or stanchion so you can take a closer look.

Teeth: Imagine our shock at discovering our newly purchased two-year-old doe had no upper incisor teeth! She had a full complement of eight front teeth on the bottom, but where did those top choppers go? Turns out that goats and sheep both simply don't have upper incisors — just a flat, toothless, pad against which their lower choppers work. Those eight bottom teeth must do all the goat's food gathering, so they've got to be in good shape. Hold the goat's head steady by the nose and gently pull or fold back her lower lip. If she's got all eight and they look solid, the teeth are okay. If any are missing, or the teeth appear loose, or have wide spaces between them, or are more than an inch long, then you're looking at an elderly girl here. We'd bypass that older goat until we had more goat experience.

Feet: Your new goat has to be able to walk from feed sources to the milking stall, so her cloven hooves had better be up to the job. Most goat keepers trim their animals' toenails from time to time, and the feet are generally in pretty decent shape. Beware of "pixie toes" — turned up, overgrown hooves. Those extra-long toenails are just as uncomfortable for the animals as claw-like toenails would be for you — and that'll cut down her mobility and milk production. Pixie toes also suggest less than adequate care for the animals, and so should rate a turn-down.

Feel each of the goat's feet — she may not particularly like this, and may try to pull away. If any foot feels especially warm, has a slight greenish tinge, or carries an unpleasant odor, this goat is most likely suffering from "foot rot." Ask! The condition is contagious, so you might as well leave this place right now. (The greenish color comes from a copper-based treatment used to counteract the problem.) If there's a hint of foot rot, when you get home you might consider taking your own shoes off in the car and carrying them into the house for scrubbing with a bleach solution. You don't want to introduce foot rot to your property, since it's difficult to eliminate.

If the goat limps, it could indicate any number of things, including a sprained ankle, having been bumped in the shoulder or hip by another goat, a limb deformity, or other foot ailments. Unless you know for sure that the limp is caused by a simple mechanical injury (such as a sprain), this trait would be grounds for refusal. Don't buy problems.

Udder: This is the part of the goat that will cause you the greatest grief or give the most satisfaction. There's a lot of variation in udders — from the high, tightly held round udder to the long, pendulous, nearly-dragging-on-the-ground type. There are udders with two teensy teats, and ones with a pair that would shame a cow. There are udders, which are firm and springy, and ones that are like flabby sponges. Here's a first rule of thumb: the udder must be evenly balanced. Both sides of the udder should be about the same size and texture. You can determine this visually, and by feeling the udder. Reach behind the goat and cup each side of the udder in your hand. It should feel body-temperature warm, soft and yielding. There should be no hard spots, extra heat, graininess, lumps or sores — which are indications of disease, possibly mastitis (infected udder). Reject any goat with signs of udder disease.

The next rule of thumb is: the udder should sit firmly high against the goat's underside. A long, droopy udder can produce a good quantity of just-fine milk — but the poor goat can get that pendulous appendage caught on wire fences, large stones, and even wind up stepping on it! The shape of the goat's udder is also an inheritable trait, so if you plan to keep daughters from this doe, you'd best avoid problems.

Finally, get a hold of each teat and test your milking skills — squeeze thumb and forefinger gently closed and then close each finger in succession. Some goats object to strangers getting this familiar when there's no grain to hold their caprine attention. Forge on anyway. Does the teat protrude slightly from the end of your hand? Milking will be easier and cleaner if the teat's tip clears your palm. If the doe has extra-large teats, feel for "backflow" — where you squeeze the teat and the milk feels as though it moves both out of the teat and back into the udder. This isn't necessarily a bad trait; it only makes milking a bit more challenging. If backflow is the goat's only problem and you take her, you can figure you're going to develop particularly strong hands over the next few months.

Past and Future

If your potential doe has passed so far, you'll need to ask about her personal health history — how old she was when first bred, how many kids she's had at each "freshening" or birthing, if she has ever produced a "freemartin" or hermaphrodite kid (not uncommon, particularly in naturally hornless goats). The more babies she can have at one time, the more you have to sell, raise up into new milkers, or put in the freezer. Remember that in order to produce milk, your doe will have to be bred every fall or winter — and those kids are one of the valuable byproducts dairy goats provide.

It's interesting to ask how much milk your potential nanny gives. I've never spoken to any goat-raiser who claimed less than a gallon daily for their does — but I've sure met a lot of goats who fall short of this amount! Most does are capable of producing a significant quantity of milk, but they must also be routinely dewormed (either with dairy wormers or by various organic methods) and fed enough to maintain their weight while still cranking out milk. The addition of molasses to feed always ups milk production somewhat — and raw, chopped pumpkin is a super milk increaser!

Most goats will drop milk production when they're moved to a new location, or stressed when being handled by strangers, so even if the goat's owner has kept perfect records, the doe's production will be less than expected. It'll pick up again after a week or two of your tender loving care. Be sure to ask about the animal's feed, milking routines, and vaccination history (have the owner write this down). If the owner has a special type of feed, ask to buy five or ten pounds so the goat has a familiar food for several days.

If this is the nanny who will provide your milk, she'll probably set you back $50 to $150. If she comes with kids, they shouldn't be more than $25 each, unless they are exceptionally fancy.

Your new goat may need to be "broke to lead," or trained to be on a leash — or she may be "broke to drag," completely without formal training. She might be most easily moved to your carry or truck by showing her a bucket of feed, or she might be so freaked by this turn of events that she's near-wild. Try to be calm and patient with this prim lady, talk evenly and gently to her, and use her given name often. It does make a difference.

Some new goat owners will pen their nannies separately for a couple weeks, while they inspect the animal for any signs of illness or health problems. If we could do only three things before we brought a new goat home, we'd ask the former owner to worm the animal in our presence so we could see how it's done, and so that any internal parasites were deceased before we got home. And we'd dip each of the goat's feet, before she touched our soil, into a solution of 25% bleach and 75% water, just to be certain there were no foot diseases coming onto my property. We'd also dust our new goat with a light coating of organic rotenone or the chemical based delousing powder — so that any stray lice or ticks wouldn't have a chance.

Last, but not least, be prepared for your new goat to be lonely and afraid for a few days. She may cry piteously (and drive you nuts), or try to be extra friendly (and drive you nuts). Be sure to milk her every twelve hours, adjusting her schedules to suit your own.

And get ready! Unless you have a household chock full of your *own* assortment of kids, prepare to be swamped by the best, freshest milk you ever tasted!

Chapter Thirteen
How to Buy Your First Sheep
(Without Getting Shorn)

Multimillionaire J. Paul Getty was once asked the secret of becoming rich. He's reported to have said, "I buy when everyone is selling, and sell when everyone is buying."

Getty's contrarian strategy could be getting a workout right now, if you were in the market for sheep — there has been an on-again off-again downturn in the industry for the past couple of years, and people are still selling. Quality ewes and lambs of commercial breeds can be found in my area for $25 to $50, a drop in cost compared to five years ago. Besides which, sheep are one of the ideal small homestead animals: they can return quality meat and fiber on an annual basis for very little cash input.

Interested? Before you put down your hard-earned money for a trio of auction ewes, you must have a clear picture of what you intend to do with sheep. Want to raise a few lambs to supplement the freezer? Produce quality wool garments? Sell butcher lambs? Your vision of what sheep can offer your farm is going to make a tremendous difference in the breed or crossbreed you buy.

The amount of land you have available for sheep will also influence your decision. If you've got five good acres, it would probably be a mistake to think you're going to produce enough commercial grade meat lambs to sustain an income.

However, five acres will keep a small flock of purebreds to be sold as breeding stock, or rare breeds, or colored wool sheep. You'll still have to cull lambs to add to your freezer. That way, you can avoid competing with a neighbor who's got 200 acres of lush pasture for commercial sheep. You can also generate a higher return per animal with rare, purebred or fancy sheep.

So which breed do you want? Larger meat producers may zoom in on Suffolk, with its heavy muscling — but you might actually prefer a smaller breed with a higher lambing percentage, such as the Finnsheep or the Polypay. You may, instead, think you'd like to take up spinning, and turn to fancy-wooled types like the Romney, Cotswold, Jacob or Karakul.

Sheep in full-wool attire.
(Photo credit: Justin Evangelista)

The only way to find out is to research what's available in your area — or seek out specialty breeders from sheep-oriented publications. Locally, you can look around and find out what breeds are dominant. It will be an indicator of which types do best in your climate and forage conditions, particularly if sheep have been there for a long time. If sheep are new to your area, go very slowly and carefully. All those other new shepherds who seem to have very clear ideas about their flocks might not have the practical experience to make informed decisions. Ask your local extension agent for the names of regional producers. Make appointments and go visit shepherds. Most sheep people are delighted to talk about their animals.

"Portrait of Bob as a lamb."
A Cheviot/Rambouillet ram who loves the camera.
(Photo credit: Justin Evangelista)

Lambs or Ewes?

If you've raised cattle or hogs, goats or chickens, none of these will prepare you fully for raising sheep. There is an old saying about "the eye of the shepherd" being the best medicine for his flock; that is, experience with the animals is the only factor that will truly keep them well.

Ewes or lambs?
(Photo credit: Justin Evangelista)

Sheep are such naturally hardy and resilient creatures that it takes a terrible illness to make one straggle along behind the flock, or lie down and be left alone. If a sheep "goes down" from a disease, it is very, very sick. If you can walk up to a normally flighty sheep and touch it, it is at death's door. Slightly sick cattle are easy to spot: an ill hog will have a temperature and act funny right away. But a sheep fading from pneumonia or worms will keep right along with the flock until it can't stand up.

This has led to a common misconception about sheep: that they just up and die for no apparent reason. One day they're well, the next they're dead. Shepherds who believe this have already missed all the signs, such as that odd twitch of the ears, an uneven couch, the slight limp, the weight loss going on unseen under a beautiful coat of wool.

What we're getting at here is that unless you already know the difference between a slightly ill sheep and a perfectly healthy one, you should not start with the most susceptible animals. You shouldn't start with lambs.

Healthy, mature ewes pretty much know what it's all about. They've been through several lambings, they've developed a certain tolerance to parasites, they're used to being manhandled by people. They won't be as flighty as lambs. They will practically show you how to take care of them.

Inspection

Your best bet is a small set of mature ewes, three-to-five-years-old, of one of the long-lived breeds. Don't buy cheap auction animals! You will spend a fortune on these "low-cost" items in vet bills. If you must buy at auction, look for the biggest, huskiest sheep, and figure that half of them will prove worthless — otherwise their former owner would have kept them.

Instead, seek your new ewes from a breeder. Ask every question you can think of about their ancestry, health, and production capabilities, including: How many lambs has the ewe had? When was she last wormed, and with what product? Has she been sick, ever? If so, how was she treated? Has she had mastitis, or been unable to produce enough milk for her lambs? What is her breeding ancestry? Why is the owner selling the sheep?

Remember when buying from sheep producers, you'll be getting their culls — the sheep they no longer want for one reason or another. The ewe in question may not have produced as well as the owner wanted, may have had several difficult births, or be unattractive in some way. However, the cull of a fine flock may be better than the premium animal of a poor flock. And you probably don't need super-producers to begin with — just a good, sound animal with several years left in her.

Ask to see the sheep separated from the rest of the flock in a small pen. Get in with the sheep, put your hands deep into the wool and feel for the ribs. If you can feel a prominent rib cage, check for the back bone and hips. If these bones are sticking out, you're looking at a severely malnourished sheep. (She could have ovine progressive pneumonia, she could have just finished raising triplets and be droopy, she could be wormy, she could be very old and have no teeth left to chew with, or she might just be unable to compete at the feeder with more aggressive animals.) Skinny sheep that are otherwise healthy might be a good deal for someone who's got feed, pasture and lots of practical experience, but if you can't tell if they're healthy or not, let them go.

Check the Udder

Have the sheep turned up on her rump so that you can take a look at her udder. If she's not pregnant and hasn't been nursing, her udder should be small with two prominent nipples. Feel it. There should be no hard spots, lumpiness or graininess. If there is, she's probably had mastitis or nursed lambs that had sore mouth disease. Reject her. It is too much effort for a beginner to raise lambs from a ewe that can't produce milk. Tiny extra odd shaped and odd-spaced teats will rarely be a problem unless they block a normal one.

If a ewe has been nursing or is pregnant, her udder should be firm and evenly balanced. If she's nursing and has a hard side or hard spot in her udder she's too sick for you to take home. Reject her for mastitis.

Check the Feet

While she's up on her backside, take a look at her hooves. They might be overgrown or trimmed; neither really matters at this moment. Pick up each hoof. If one is hotter than the others, something's wrong. It could be a thorn in her foot, or it could be foot rot. Reject her for this reason. If her feet seem to be fine, as a final check you can sniff them. Foot rot has a particularly pungent and unpleasant odor that you can't miss. If the hooves look really closely and neatly trimmed, with a tinge of greenish color about them, chances are that she has recently been treated for a case of foot rot — the green color comes from a copper-based medication. Ask. Treatment on this particular farm could be prophylactic, trying to *prevent* disease rather than *cure* it. Never buy a footsore or limping animal, for fear of bringing foot rot on to your property. Any hint of this disease is sufficient reason for refusal to purchase. A sheep without the ability to move around is not going to do well and can spread foot rot to the rest of your flock.

Teeth and Wool

Determining the age of a ewe by looking at her mouth is a bit more complicated than we can cover in detail here, but take a look at her teeth anyway. Separate her lips and make sure she has a row of six to eight teeth on the bottom that meet evenly with her upper pad. Sheep have no upper incisor teeth. Broken, missing, extra long, or badly aligned teeth indicate the possibility of great age in the ewe, or of feeding difficulties to come (since she can't chew well). Bad teeth make a sheep iffy, and I'd probably reject her for it.

Finally, look hard and long at the sheep's wool. Feel its texture. Tug a little bit out by wrapping it around your finger and slowly pulling. Is this the color and texture you want? If you plan to make rugs from your sheep's wool, you'll probably want a coarse-textured fiber. If sweaters and scarves are your choice, go with a finer-textured wool. If you're looking at crossbred sheep, the only way to determine what you're getting is to feel each animal's fleece.

Medical and Family History

Now's the time to talk health and family history on these ewes. Some producers keep extensive on-paper records; some just try to remember every animal in the flock. The paper records are probably more consistently reliable.

If you can, find out if this ewe has ever had a rectal or uterine prolapse (where the lining of the rectum or uterus protrudes from the body). If so, this is a good reason to reject her. That trait is inheritable, and you don't want your future sheep to have prolapses.

Has she been a good mother, raising her lamb or lambs by herself? Get specific details. If this ewe has any Suffolk blood and has produced a crippled lamb, she may be carrying a genetic abnormality known as spider syndrome. The malformed lambs generally die at birth or shortly after. Don't buy a problem.

Basically, you're looking for sound sheep. They don't have to be valuable, high producers, or of brilliant colors. You need to find hardy sheep that will survive a year or two of your own (let's be honest) incompetence. It happens to all new shepherds, and most of us will be embarrassed to tell you the awful, terrible things we did to sheep during our first two years.

You'll learn an incredible amount of information just from making mistakes. Sheep will die from what you did — or what you didn't — do. We have, on prominent display in our kitchen, two sheep skulls. One is of a market-weight weather lamb; the other is from an older ewe. Both of these animals died from intestinal parasites because we didn't deworm them on time. We keep them to remind us to worm the sheep. We haven't lost one to worms since.

You see, your education has a price. We felt bad enough losing these two commercial sheep because of our ignorance, but imagine how much worse we'd have felt if these were the last of an extremely rare breed, or if they had cost us $500 apiece! Cut your losses by buying healthy but average stock.

The lesson for all beginners is to start small and grow slowly. In a couple of years, you'll know more precisely what you can and cannot do with sheep. You'll know when yours are healthy and when they're not, and whether you really like raising sheep or not.

It just might become a habit.

Chapter Fourteen
Lambing Season: A Dialogue

(There's twelve years of sheep experience crammed into this chapter. Pay attention.)

Lambing season — the birthing time of sheep — has always been an extremely trying time for us. From the very start, with our first pregnant ewe, it's been that way. We feel responsible for the new lives coming into the world, probably more than the mother sheep, who seem to take the whole delivery process pretty much matter-of-factly.

Nick: Well, it's almost January. Lambing season should be starting soon.

Anita: Pretty quick.

Nick: I hate lambing season!

Anita: Why? Lambing season means new sheep — sheep we can sell, sheep we can put in the freezer. Lambing season is good.

Nick: I know, I know.

Anita: Money! Food! Money! Food!

Nick: Okay, okay, I understand.

Anita: So ...?

Nick: So, I can't help it. I've been traumatized by all the horrible birthing experiences I've waded through over the years. Want to see my scarred psyche?

Anita: Not on an empty stomach.

Lamb!
(Photo credit: Justin Evangelista)

Nick: I'm serious.

Anita: Uh huh.

Nick: You were lucky enough to be away from the farm for most of the more grisly incidents.

Anita: Probably helped that those old Scrooges expected me to be at work, or something. Maybe I just had good timing.

Nick: My clock must be slow then.

Anita: I've always thought that. I think I'll have a cup of coffee.

Nick: Pour me one, too.

Anita: Like you need more caffeine in your system. Is there a full moon tonight?

Nick: I crave coffee!

Anita: Here's your java. Stay away from the power tools.

Nick: Um. But, you know, I do have a problem with lambing season.

Anita: I see. Why do I suddenly feel like Sigmund Freud? So, name something really bad that's happened during lambing season.

Nick: Well, first off, how about all the lambs that just plain died after they were born? Because we didn't know what we were doing. There's nothing like death to put you on edge.

Anita: We lost some lambs, but we learned from our mistakes.

Nick: So, now I'm more aware of all the things that can go wrong. Great! More stuff to worry about, right? Has the mother ewe accepted the baby or babies? Is she producing enough milk? Has the baby found the udder and nursed? Has the baby had its first bowel movement — passed its meconium ... see, I remember the words — or does it need an enema?

Anita: You want to give *every* lamb an enema. It's weird.

Nick: No, I don't.

Anita: Do so.

Nick: Do not. I only give enemas to lambs I think may be stressed. It's an acceptable procedure.

Anita: But you think nearly every lamb is stressed when it's born. They have built-in systems that take care of bodily functions on their own.

Nick: I get nervous.

Anita: And then you wake me at three o'clock in the morning to help you give a perfectly healthy lamb an enema. *That* should make you nervous, buddy.

Nick: Hey, we don't lose lambs from meconium retention anymore, do we?

Anita: No, but —

Nick: I must be doing something right.

Anita: Or the lambs are.

Nick: Look, if a lamb retains its meconium, its system becomes clogged up. The lamb dies. It's in that sheep book we have. I didn't make it up. It's easier to give them an enema than try to save them once they've started to sink. That's only common sense.

Anita: All right, if you say so.

Nick: I do.

Anita: Got any other lambing horrors tucked away?

Nick: Sure. Remember the time I read that James Herriot story about one of the difficult lambing seasons he went through as a vet? I said something like, "I hope this isn't an omen." Three days later, I had two lambs being born at once — out of one ewe. Two lamb heads coming out at the same time. Wedged nice and tight. How did they manage that?

You, as one might expect, were in town. I, as one might expect, didn't know what to do. I called you on the phone. You said, "Get them out." Great advice. Get them out! Like I couldn't figure that out. I went back, and fiddled with the babies for twenty minutes before I could tell whose legs belonged to whom. I had to get my hand in there with the lambs, which was a miracle in itself, before I was able to get them unstuck, to ease one of them forward. I thought I was going to rip the poor ewe in half. The ewe was jumping around. My hand got crunched and twisted. It was not fun.

Anita: But you did it.

Nick: Yes, I did. Of course, one of the lambs was dead by the time I got them unjammed.

Anita: That wasn't your fault.

Nick: Recall what happened to the other lamb?

Anita: The ewe —

Nick: The stupid ewe ....

Anita: The ewe sat on it two days later, and —

Nick: It died, too.

Anita: That wasn't your fault either.

Nick: But the lambs were dead. That's what sticks with me.

Anita: I see.

Nick: And how about Old Fatty?

Chapter Fourteen
Lambing Season: A Dialogue

141

Anita: The ewe that came down with ketosis?

Nick: Yeah, the "pregnant ewe" disease. The ewe was too old, too fat, and too pregnant — she had triplets in her. It was too much for her system to take. She had a toxic build-up in her system, and down she went.

Anita: Remember that kind of syrupy sweet smell on her breath?

Nick: Uh huh. Ketosis usually kills them in a few days, but I kept her alive for eight weeks, until she was ready to lamb. I fed her by hand five times a day — that paste I made in the blender from vegetables, garlic, grain, molasses — all kinds of stuff. I also had to move her around the barn to keep her clean. It was like taking care of an old lady invalid — a *wooly* old lady invalid. She finally had three lambs. The first two were born dead.

Anita: But the last one was alive.

Nick: And Old Fatty died right after that. Her liver gave out from all the stress she went through.

Anita: You kept her alive longer than anyone else might have. Long enough for her to have one live, healthy baby. In a way, it was a miracle. Didn't we call her "Grace" — short for "Amazing Grace"? You should be pleased.

Nick: I guess it would be okay if the awful stuff ended there. But I've had a lot more hard deliveries to contend with, you know.

Anita: Actually, the sheep had the hard deliveries — you were just there to help out. How many would you say, Doctor Doolittle?

Nick: A bunch. Twenty? At least that.

Anita: Somebody had to do it.

Nick: I'm not cut out for it. I'm from Los Angeles.

Anita: Silly person.

Nick: Remember 181 — the ewe with the dead lamb in her? The bloated dead lamb. What did the veterinary book say about that problem? "Call a vet to remove it." We couldn't afford a vet. I had to take it out myself. How? I pulled it apart — piece by stinking piece — until I could get the main hunk of guck out. The baby didn't even have discernable body parts anymore. Talk about gross. It was ripe, to say the least. The smell was unique. Then, the ewe started bleeding, and I was sure I'd killed her. Luckily, it was just old brownish blood left over in the dead placenta — not bright red fresh stuff that would have shown an arterial leak. What a mess. I felt like Jack the Ripper.

Anita: She pulled through, though.

Nick: I don't know how. Not because of my light touch. It took four full hours to get that job done. A vet would have gotten paid. I ruined my best pair of jeans.

Anita: Didn't 181 have two healthy babies next season?

Nick: That's right, two healthy babies she didn't take care of. I had to catch her and hold her still every time the lambs needed to nurse. Talk about labor intensive!

Anita: She finally took them.

Nick: After about three weeks of wrestling around the barn with her. What a creep. Essentially, it was World Wrestling Federation with a walking wooly baby bottle. I could have smacked her in the head with a baseball bat. Then, one day, something clicked in her brain, and she started taking care of them. She actually did a pretty good job, too. But before that...!

Anita: Well, then, that wasn't so bad. A happy ending.

Nick: What about all the rejected babies we couldn't get the ewes to take?

Anita: You raised them.

Nick: Yes, I raised them. I got to be mom.

Anita: That wasn't so bad, was it?

Nick: Five, six feedings a day. The last one at four in the morning. Bad? I thought I was done with that nonsense after our kids turned into humans.

Anita: At least you didn't have to diaper the lambs.

Nick: Big deal. One year I was bottle feeding ten lambs at once. At least, our own kids came two years apart.

Anita: You can't tell me you don't like taking care of lambs.

Nick: They get attached to me.

Anita: They get attached to *you?* That's funny. You'd adopt them legally, if I'd let you.

Nick: I'm not that bad.

Anita: Oh? For a long time, you refused to sell lambs you took care of. That was you, wasn't it?

Nick: Musta been somebody else. But you couldn't get me to eat them. That would be cannibalism.

Anita: So, how many non-dinners do you think you've hand-raised?

Nick: Let's see. There was Lamby and Baby and Gracie and Skunkie and Timmy and Hughie and Thing and Suicide and Dumpling and Wiggie and Bug and Poopie and Birdie and Freda and Norman and Buddy and Klaus and Freck and —

Anita: You're not supposed to name them!

Nick: I name them to keep track of them at feeding time.

Anita: Why not call them things like "lambchop" or "burger" or "stewmeat"? Couldn't you just number them? Or would that be too simple?

Nick: Names happen.

Anita: Oh, really?

Nick: We sell lambs now, don't we?

Anita: And then you mope around for a day or two — like your own children were going off to live with strangers.

Nick: Hmph.

Anita: It would be easier on you if you'd look on it as a business, rather than a buddy-generating system.

Nick: Me and Popeye am what we am.
Anita: You know, sometimes you ask for trouble.
Nick: How's that?

Sheep are fully insulated from the cold.
(Photo credit: Justin Evangelista)

Anita: For instance, the time you kept that abandoned lamb in the house.
Nick: Peanut?
Anita: Yes, Peanut.
Nick: He was only two-days-old.
Anita: You could have kept him in a pen in the barn. He would have been warm and safe. But no! You had to keep him with you. And, at night, you let him sleep with you on the living room couch.
Nick: So?

Chapter Fourteen
Lambing Season: A Dialogue

Anita: What did Peanut do?

Nick: I forget.

Anita: You forget? Let me jog your memory. In the middle of the night, he climbed on your head. And then he ...?

Nick: I'd rather not talk about it.

Anita: He went pee-pee, that's what he did!

Nick: Oh, he was just a baby.

Anita: Right. As I recall, when you woke up in the morning, you had that cool 1950s wet head look. And there was that earthy odor...

Nick: Hey, I washed my hair, didn't I?

Anita: Great backup plan. Sometimes you ask for it.

Nick: Well, maybe sometimes. But what about the weak lambs, the ones that wouldn't have made it without special handling. Like the babies I had to tube feed. Shoving that plastic tube down their throats into their stomachs. Puffing into it to be certain it wasn't in a lung. Talk about harrowing! One mistake, and you fill their lungs with milk.

Anita: You did it right. The lambs survived.

Nick: How is beyond me.

Anita: You survived, too.

Nick: I almost forgot to mention Suicide, the lamb with the terrible bloat. I had to put a tube down into his stomach to get out gas. Then, I had to suck on the tube to get the gas flow going. I also sucked up a mouth-full of lamb stomach liquid. I'll tell you something, it won't ever replace Coke.

Anita: At least not in the major markets.

Nick: Now, do you see why I have such a problem with lambing season?

Anita: I suppose. I concede lambing season hasn't exactly been a jolly barrel of laughs. Just the same, every year more and more of our lambs survived. Last year — for the first time in a handful of years — we lost only one. And it was born dead. We must be learning something.

Nick: I suppose so. Still, I can't get this nagging feeling of impending doom out of my mind. It hovers there — like smog.

Anita: Get over it.

Nick: That's easy for you to say.

Anita: It is. I'll say it again. Get over it.

Nick: The question is, why do I keep putting myself through this lambing stuff?

Anita: Sheesh, what part did you miss? You love sheep! No one who didn't love sheep would put up with such agony. And besides, you're stuck with it.

Nick: Oh, yah. I forgot.

Chapter Fifteen
Of Snakes and Sheep

Nick: It happened our very first fall lambing.

It was a warm September night when Anita and I decided to look in on our ewes. We had two pregnant Polypay girls who were starting to resemble major tug boats, and, having had only a couple lambs during our first experience with lambing earlier in the year, we were filled with the nervous expectation of beginners. It was as if we had to be looking at the sheep when their babies came out, or something would doubtlessly go wrong. Deep down, I think I was harboring this secret conviction that sheep never had babies before humans came along — that lambing was invented by people. Before that, sheep just sort of subdivided like amoebas.

Anyway, with these cheerful thoughts finely etched into my mind, Anita and I entered the barn.

The scene seemed to be status quo. Some ewes were standing, some were laying. Everyone was chewing cud in that relaxed, matter-of-fact way sheep have when they're contented (when thoughts of shots and shearing are far away). The Polypays were still blimps. Then I noticed a ewe standing off to one side in a shadowy corner. The animal was facing away from the rest of the flock, head down, as though harboring some deep, dark secret, which she was doing her best to hide from us.

An experienced, long-time shepherd might have looked at this scene and saw it for what it was. Not me. It never occurred to me what was up. Hit me with that two-by-four.

"That's odd," I remarked. "I wonder what's wrong with that ewe?"

"Let's get hold of her and take a look," Anita said.

We didn't have to catch her. When we got close, we saw the new lamb, still damp, huddled behind its mother's protective form.

My wife and I stared in surprise.

"That's a lamb!" I said.

"Yes, it is," Anita replied.

"That ewe isn't pregnant."

Anita sighed. "Well, she's sure done a good job of faking it."

"But —!"

"I guess she was pregnant."

"Well, she didn't *look* pregnant," I said.

"Complain to *her*, not me."

I shrugged. Then, I started to get revved up. This was still pretty much new stuff for me.

"Well, let's get going. We'd better get them into the lambing pen before anything goes wrong."

"Calm down," Anita said. "Let's take this a step at a time. Is the pen clean?"

I nodded. "I cleaned it three days ago. I put in fresh hay. Come and look for yourself."

We walked over to the enclosure. I didn't see the black snake curled up in the center of the lambing pen right away. My brain had to assimilate what I was viewing. My first thought was, "Who the heck dumped that hose in there?"

"That's a snake!" Anita said, without hesitation.

I could hear the information beep, beep, beeping through the circuits inside my head, trying to sort itself into a useful response.

Finally, my mouth fell open.

"What's it doing in there?"

The snake looked up at us with a kind of blunt-faced defiance. Its darting tongue seemed to be a warning to keep away.

"It looks as if it thinks it's found a home in there," Anita observed.

"Great, fine!" I said. "Stupid snake!"

"It can't stay in there."

"What should we do?"

"Well..."

"I'll get the shovel."

"You can't kill it!" Anita said. "Black snakes are good. They keep away poisonous snakes and mice."

I ran a tense hand through my hair.

"Well, what then? If we just scare if off, it might come back after we leave. That's a big snake. Can a snake like that kill a lamb?"

"I don't know," Anita admitted.

"What do you suggest?" I asked.

Anita looked at me blankly.

"You'll have to catch it and take it away," she said, matter-of-factly.

"*What?*" I said, in disbelief.

"It's the only way."

"I can't do that."

"Sure you can," she said. "It's just a snake."

"If it's so easy, you do it!"

Anita smiled.

"I'm a girl. Girls don't have to touch snakes."

"Yeah? Well, I'm a coward. Cowards don't have to touch snakes either."

Anita frowned. I hate it when she frowns.

"You don't want that snake to kill that little lamb, do you? Do you think that poor little baby can defend itself?"

I bowed my head.

"No."

"Well, you'll have to do something."

"Okay, okay. I'll take the snake out," I said, a feeling of doom sweeping over me. I pulled on my gloves. "Why me?" I groaned. "I mean, I don't remember reading anything in the sheep book about having to do mortal combat with dinosaurs."

I opened the lambing pen gate.

Anita stepped back. "Be careful."

"Thanks," I said. "These things don't eat people, do they? I'm not ready to become part of the food chain."

"It's not a python," Anita pointed out. "Black snakes aren't big enough to eat humans. But keep it away from your neck. I think they can squeeze pretty hard."

"Oh, fine! It won't eat me. It'll just strangle me to death."

The snake, inky, jelly-bean eyes regarding me warily, waited in silent expectation. Its tongue flickered nervously.

"Okay, snake," I said, "be nice."

My mind raced. Which end would I take hold of? Where do you grab a snake's head so that it can't munch on your arm? I quickly decided on the tail, the farthest point from the mouth. I'm not completely stupid.

I took hold of the snake firmly and pulled. At first, it resisted in a mild but muscularly insistent way. It was cool and hard to the touch, one long muscle, unwinding stiffly. But I yanked, and the coil yielded grudgingly. And it just kept unwinding and unwinding and unwinding. All six feet of it. It was about as large as a black snake can get. Of course.

Feeling threatened, the snake came to life. It's white lined, lipless mouth gaping cavernously, it twisted up with lightening speed, ready to sink its sharp teeth into my offending fingers. With equal swiftness, I dropped the reptile back on the floor. Anita flew to the far side of the barn, shrieking, sending bewildered sheep bounding off in all directions. I jumped away.

Certain the snake would head for shelter, and then just come back later, I kicked myself for losing it. But, to my surprise, it stayed put, spiraling into a defensive mound, ready for a fight. I seized a nearby rake, and thrust it on to the snake's head, pinning it down firmly in the hay. It thrashed about wildly, but it couldn't get away.

With my free hand, I wrapped my fingers around the gyrating tail and dragged the thing out of the pen and across the barn floor toward the door. I had to get it outside. I banged squarely into the barn door and shoved it open with a mindless desperation usually reserved for bad dreams about being chased by giant cartons of milk. The snake, strung out like a wet noodle, seemed disoriented by the ordeal, which state I hoped would continue for some time. But as soon as we emerged into the night air, it came to life again.

What now? I thought. The basic plan was to get rid of the creature, yet do it efficiently, so it wouldn't return. But how do you intimidate a snake? You can't threaten to break its kneecaps.

Suddenly I had an idea. If a person could manage to grab a snake by its tail, and then swing it around in a circle like a lasso, that might just render the little snake head, full of its sharp, snaky teeth, harmless. It probably couldn't do much coiling and squeezing either.

Inspiration!

Centrifugal force!

Science in action!

And I already had the snake by the tail.

I began twirling the reptile over my head, around and around, faster and faster. And, sure enough, my plan worked like a charm. Snakes can't do anything when all their blood is rushing into their nose.

Anita peered out from the barn.

"What are you doing?" she asked in disbelief.

"I'll explain later," I shouted.

Amid the sounds of my spouse's sudden raucous laughter, I loped off into the moonless night, swinging the snake for all I was worth above me.

So this is shepherding, I mused.

About a hundred yards from the barn, I decided it was time for the snake and me to part company. Giving it one last extra strong whip, I let go. The snake flew away.

The next moment, I heard the swishy crack and snap of a heavy object crashing through a clump of bushes.

When I arrived back at the barn, Anita had already ensconced the sheep and her baby in the lambing pen. The ewe was feasting deliberately on a mouthful of alfalfa; the lamb, tail wiggling happily, was nursing on a full udder.

"Well?" Anita asked. "What happened?"

"Piece of cake," I said. "The last time the offender was seen, he was headed south like a pinwheel."

"Oh?"

"I'll bet he has a real good headache in the morning."

And that was that. The snake didn't come back to the lambing pen.

Ever.

But I'll tell you, I hope I never have to do that again. I'd rather trim a thousand sheep hooves with cuticle scissors.

Chapter Sixteen
Nick's Lamb Story

Nick: The lamb I found up on the hillside abandoned by her mother became our first success at saving abandoned lambs.

I named her Lamby.

Lamby.

Pretty sickening, huh? Well, what should I have called her? Mozart? Recreational vehicle? Spike? Oatmeal? Rodan?

She was a lamb, so Lamby it was.

Anita told me, "Don't name them. You name them, and you can never eat them."

I named her Lamby.

Lamby spent the first two months of her life living in our kitchen, as she was too small to be put out alone with the other sheep.

She was a curious little animal. She watched television, rode in our car (her head sticking out the window like a dog's) and generally turned our house into a barn, if you know what I mean.

I put up with her bathroom habits. I was her Mom, after all. Eventually, though, Lamby and her messes grew too big to keep in the house, and she joined the flock — which was traumatic for *me*. But you have to know when to let go of the children, don't you?

At first, Lamby was standoffish. She had no idea what those

ugly, woolly things that couldn't speak English or drive cars were. Every time a ewe came near her, she ran and hid between my legs.

In time, though, she started to get the hang of sheep stuff.

When she was two-years-old, Lamby had her first baby. I wondered what kind of mother she would be with me as a role model for motherhood — and I was a bit worried, but she turned out to be a great mother. She was super attentive. Also, incredibly protective. More than one dog that came too close to her baby received the torpedo treatment, and she'd keep nailing them if they weren't immediately dispersed by her onslaught.

After that, she became a crabby old grump. She'd always suffer us to handle her, but she made it clear with squirms and foot stomps that she wasn't enjoying it.

For me, the whole experience of raising a lamb from day one was a turning point for my brain. Before Lamby, I looked on our sheep basically as machines and merchandise. Afterwards, I began seeing them as living, thinking creatures with feelings and individual personalities.

Of course, maybe this makes me a flawed businessperson. To be good in the livestock trade, I think, you have to keep a certain distance between you and your animals. But what can I say? I'm stuck. I like the darn things now.

And it all started with one abandoned lamb.

Chapter Seventeen
Rocky: A Horse Story

Nick: In times of trouble, in the country, there often appears to be a powerful universal equation at work, that the degree of one's disaster is in equal proportion to one's inability to seek assistance.

At least, it seems like it.

Anyway, this was how it stacked up when our horse Rocky came down with colic. Nearly two feet of Arctic-blast-driven winter snow fell abruptly and unexpectedly on the Ozarks — a light dusting of snow had been predicted — the night it happened.

We were utterly snow bound, cut off from the world.

And very much on our own.

✖✖✖✖✖✖

But of course, it all started rather simply. Doesn't it always start that way?

The early part of the day had been warm and sunny, for early January — maybe up to a toasty forty-five degrees. This was absolutely spring-like — sweater weather we call it — after countless drab, overcast days that hovered in the teens and twenties. It almost seemed as though winter was on the wane.

Almost.

Our livestock were enjoying the "elevated" temperature. They basked lazily in the bright sun, soaking up the unaccustomed warmth of the bare earth. The barnyard was a tangled mob of sheep, goats, chickens, geese, ducks and a horse.

One horse.

Rocky.

Rocky was a big, dark brown Morgan. And old — considerably over twenty when we got him. He was one of those sweet farm animals whose long life had been a constant move from one owner to another — a four-legged foster child, just like in *Black Beauty*. He'd been given to us, free of charge, by some folks who'd sold their farm and were suddenly out of the livestock tending profession.

Rocky — 22-years-old.
(Photo credit: Justin Evangelista)

He was an even-tempered old guy, steady and tolerant of even the most clumsy human hands. When he was a youngster — we were told — he'd been a champion show horse, valued in the multi-thousands of dollars. Then, somehow, he'd been accidentally gelded — which pretty much dropped his horse flesh value to almost zip. No offspring from him! It was at this point that his life of musical farms began.

On the day in question, he'd been our horse for about two years.

✖✖✖✖✖✖

Around eight o'clock in the evening, I went out to the barnyard to set out hay for the sheep, goats, and Rocky. I did this every night in the winter. The temperature had dropped considerably from what it had been during the day, but I didn't think anything of it. When it got dark, it got cold. That was normal. But as I spread the feed around among the pushing throng of animal bodies, I suddenly became aware of the occasional snow flake floating noiselessly, innocently to the ground.

A portent.

At the same time, I saw there was something wrong with Rocky. Not only was he not eating — he was usually the first one into whatever food we put out, hay or grain — greedily and forcefully guarding his staked out portion, but here he was, standing off to one side, near the barn door, his head down.

I walked over to him.

"How you doing, Rock?" I asked.

His breathing came heavily in labored groans. I knew the horse, and this wasn't right.

I went in the house, and told Anita.

"Something's wrong with Rocky," I said.

"Like what?" she replied, looking up from a book.

I described what I'd observed.

"This could be bad," Anita said, who knew horses much better than I did.

"How bad?"

"It sounds like he might have colic."

"Isn't colic basically a stomach ache? Something that babies get?"

"Colic can kill horses."

"Oh."

"If that's what he has, he's blocked up, got a kinked bowel — can't go poop. And that gives him a stomach ache you wouldn't believe."

"And that can kill him?"

"Horses aren't people. For all their size and strength, it doesn't take much to do them in."

"Well," I said, "let's go out and take a look at him together. Then, we can make a decision about what to do. Okay?"

The snow was coming down in heavy curtains of white when we set out from the house. The wind was blowing steadily from the North. The ground was already blanketed by almost an inch of clinging icy powder.

"It's really starting to come down now," I said.

"The weather report on the radio promised light snow for tonight," Anita remarked.

"Looks like they lied again."

Rocky was nowhere in sight when we arrived in the barnyard. Anita shot the beam of our flashlight around the enclosure. Startled sheep and goats milled around nervously.

"Where'd he go?"

We looked inside the big barn. He wasn't there.

"I'll check the milking area," I said. I went to a little side enclosure.

There was Rocky, laying uncomfortably in the middle of the room.

"In here," I shouted.

Anita came over, took one look at the animal, and shook her head.

"He's got colic," she decided. "Look how his stomach's kinda bulging." She touched his side. The horse groaned loudly. "See how tender he is there? He's in a bad way."

"But how?" I asked. "Where'd he get colic?"

Anita thought. "We wormed him this morning. Remember?"

I nodded.

"I don't know why, but it must have something to do with that. That's all I can think of."

"Wonderful! We try to make him healthy, and we kill him."

"You just never know."

"So," I said, "what do we do now?"

"I'll go in the house and check my vet books," Anita decided. "But first we have to get him on his feet and walking. Laying down is the worst thing for him. When the pain gets too bad, he may start rolling on his back and kicking. If he does that, he could twist a bowel. Then he's a dead horse for sure. They call it torsion. It's a slow, painful way to go, too. A vet would just put him down then."

I took hold of Rocky's halter and pulled.

"Come on, horse," I grunted, straining to get him up. "I can't do this by myself."

"He doesn't want to get up because he feels so bad," Anita said.

"You're telling me. When we're done with him, you can take care of my hernia."

I yanked again. "Up, Rock. Get up."

Finally, reluctantly, the horse stood up.

"Now lead him around," Anita directed. "Keep him walking. And, whatever you do, don't let him lay down."

"Tell him that. He's bigger than me."

"Well, do your best."

Holding on to the horse, I started forward.

"Okay, Rocky, let's dance."

Anita headed back to the house. "I'll see what we can do for him," she said over her shoulder.

"Don't take too long," I called, as she disappeared. "I'm scared of the dark."

A couple laps around the narrow barn enclosure proved too confining. The milking stand was in the way. The horse bumped against the walls, making unhappy sounds.

"This isn't working," I decided. "We'll have to go outside."

I led Rocky out into the open. The snow, now falling with a determined aggressiveness, was building up quickly.

I held out my gloved hand, catching numerous errant flakes in their downward plunge.

"This is a light snow?" I said. "From the look of things, Rocky, you and me might end up being an anthropological find five-thousand-years from now."

I brushed the snow off my face.

"Time to move."

We walked.

Around the barnyard.

Over and over and over again.

Foot prints over foot prints.

Without stopping.

Finally, Anita returned.

"Well...?" I said.

"He has colic," she said.

"Okay. He has colic."

"And he needs a vet."

"And...?"

"And — nothing. The books say to call a vet."

"That's all?"

Anita shrugged. "There isn't a vet available in three counties, anyway — I called all six of them — the storm. No answers. When a horse is that bad off, there isn't a lot you can do without vet skills."

"We can't just let him die."

"No."

I looked around at the mounting layer of snow.

"No one's coming out here."

Anita shook her head.

"Not unless you know of a vet with a helicopter or a flying saucer. I just heard on the radio there's already close to a foot of snow between us and town. And they expect maybe another foot to fall by morning."

"I'd say we're on our own."

Suddenly Rocky decided to lay down in the snow.

"Get him up! Get him up!" Anita shouted.

I pulled hard on the horse's halter. I even tugged on his mane. He went down, anyway, and rolled over on his back, kicking out his legs in pain. He almost whacked me, but I jumped back just in time.

"See what I mean?" Anita said. "We have to get him up again. He'll twist a bowel for sure if he keeps this up."

After a moment, Rocky returned to a sitting position, and I was able to coax him back on to his feet.

"Poor guy," Anita said.

"So, what now?" I asked.

Anita thought for a bit.

"We have to keep him on his feet and walking," she said. "That in itself might eventually stimulate a bowel movement."

"But if that's not enough?"

"I was thinking — maybe we can force him to eat something that might loosen him up."

"Like...?"

"I'm not sure yet."

The horse tried to pull away from me again.

"Uh oh," I said, "I have to start walking Rocky around some more. He'll be back on the ground if I don't."

Anita nodded. "Okay. I'll go in the house and see what I can find for the horse to eat."

Rocky and I moved off into the darkness.

The snow continued to fall relentlessly around us.

❆❆❆❆❆❆

Sometime later, Anita returned carrying a covered metal bowl. Rocky and I stopped.

"Finally," I said, sagging. "I'm pooped. Walking round in the cold is tiring."

"I tried to hurry," Anita explained. "It took a while, but I think I have a mixture of things that just might do the horse some good."

"What's in it?"

"Well, I started with bran for fiber, added some feed molasses for taste, and finished with a cup of olive oil for greasing up Rocky's insides. It mixed together real nicely, too, all thick and goopy. If this doesn't get his tummy jumping, nothing will."

"Sounds yummy," I said.

"Rocky won't like having to eat this stuff," Anita said. "But he has to anyway. Let's take him in the barn. He won't have any room to escape from us in there."

I nodded.

"Come on, Rock," I said. "Let's get this over with."

Inside the barn, I backed Rocky up against a wall.

"Okay," I said, "what do we do now?"

Anita passed me the bowl.

"You give him this stuff."

"Me?"

"You have to force his mouth open, shove the mixture in, and keep him from spitting it out."

"Me?"

"I don't want him biting my fingers off," Anita said.

"I don't want him biting *my* fingers off either."

"I need all my fingers for typing."

"I need mine for —"

"Picking your nose?"

"I type, too."

"You only use one finger for typing, and you know it."

"Yeah, but what if he bites off that finger?"

"All right, don't feed Rocky. So who's going to do it? He'll probably die if he doesn't get this stuff."

"I — I..." I sighed. "Okay, okay, I'll do it. I'll do it."

I took a handful of the oily bran-molasses, forced open Rock's mouth with my free hand and shoved the mess in. The horse took it surprisingly well, which I'm sure was more to do with his kindly nature than my "light" touch with animals. He chewed and chewed, managing to down most of what I fed to him.

"Done," I said, after I'd repeated the process a dozen times. "And I still have all my fingers. Now what?"

Anita looked in the pan.

"I'll go in and mix up another batch. You'll have to feed Rocky again in a few hours."

"Can I go in, too?" I asked.

"Of course not," Anita said. "You have to keep walking the horse."

"Oh."

164

❀❀❀❀❀❀

Rocky and I trudged across our snow-covered field, kicking up eruptions of white in our wake. The snow fell with a whispering hiss as it filtered through nearby bare tree limbs. I had no idea how late it was. There was no moon, no stars to track our silent course.

We just walked.

And walked.

And walked.

And walked.

And walked.

Occasionally, Rocky would flop down, rolling and moaning, but I'd get him up a minute later, and we'd be on our way again.

❀❀❀❀❀❀

Finally I heard Anita calling, and we headed back to the barn.

"More bran and molasses for Rocky," Anita announced.

"What time is it?" I asked weakly.

"One-thirty in the morning."

"Is that all?" I said. "I feel like I've been doing this for a hundred-thousand-years."

"You look pooped."

"No, I was pooped five hours ago. Now I'm the stuff even dead people feel sorry for."

Anita gave me a quick hug.

"How's Rocky?"

"Well, he's not trying to go down so much. But he hasn't done any horsy business. So, I don't know."

"How long do you think you can keep going?"

I shrugged.

"I guess if it's a matter of saving the horse's life or having to process a huge pile of dog food tomorrow morning, I can probably go for most of the night."

"Well, let's take Rocky back in the barn and feed him," Anita suggested. "Then, I'll walk him for a while."

I shook my head.

"No, I'd rather do it myself," I said. "I'll have enough to feel bad about if Rocky doesn't make it, without taking on guilt for letting you walk around in a snow storm in the middle of the night."

"You dope," Anita muttered.

The night stretched on.

Rocky and I resumed our trek. I wrapped myself in an old wool blanket Anita brought out for me; so, if nothing else, I wasn't particularly cold. After a while, my mind kind of numbed over, emptying of everything except the thought to take another step.

Stopping here and there to rest, I stared up into the unremitting fall from above.

The snow clung stubbornly to everything.

Rocky and I eventually ended up back in the barn.

I had to rest.

The horse, too. He looked as worn out as I felt.

"Okay, Rock," I said slowly. "I'm going to sit in the corner for a couple minutes and rest my eyes. Then, we'll get back to work."

When I awoke, light from the morning sun was streaming into the barn. It painted the landscape in faded pastels. The sky was pale blue tinged with streaks of red.

Morning?

Surprise.

The storm had finally petered out, but not without giving us its best shot. There was a good twenty inches of snow on the ground.

I jumped to my feet, shaking the cob webs out of my head.

"Rocky?" I shouted, expecting the worst.

The horse was in the barnyard, quietly munching on a flake of hay that protruded stubbornly through the snow. Two huge, slightly oily mounds of steamy manure were spread out triumphantly behind him. The piles were peppered with bot fly larva, huge, whitish things, all dead. No wonder he'd had a stomach ache.

I rubbed Rocky's nose.

"You did it, old horse," I said quietly. "You're going to be okay now."

Shaking his head, Rocky turned toward me and snorted. His breath formed a swirling fog around his nostrils.

"Go back to eating," I said.

Did any of Anita's and my ministrations actually do any good? Was Rocky as bad off as we thought he was, or would he have gotten better on his own anyway? To be honest, I have no idea. So, don't put this story down to sure fire cures. We did what we did because we had no other choices.

And maybe it worked. Anyway, the horse didn't die.

Would I do the whole thing all over again?

Sure.

If I had to.

Throwing my blanket over my shoulder, I plodded through the knee deep snow back to the house.

Chapter Eighteen
Working Horses
(...Well, Ponies)

If you have children on the homestead, it will be nearly inevitable. One day, you'll have to get a pony. City kids get a bicycle. Country kids get a pony.

The pony will be ridden day-and-night for about two weeks, until the juvenile attention-span wanes. After that, it will stand around, eye you angrily when you go to the barnyard, and stomp any other animal in its way when grain is put down in the feeders. It will gain weight on dry grass fields, and rub its backside on your young fruit trees until it breaks off all the lower branches.

There used to be only two types of commonly available farm ponies: Shetlands and Welsh ponies. The smaller of the two, at about 3-feet tall at the shoulder, Shetlands originated in (drum roll) the Shetland Islands, a stretch of rough rock in the cold northern ocean off of Scotland. Everything that comes from the Shetland Islands has three built-in features: (1) innate hardiness against the cold; (2) highly efficient food conversion into fat; (3) natural frustration that it won't grow very tall.

The first two features make Shetlands an ideal small horse for very poor soil and rough country — these animals can do well on land that would "starve a goose," as the saying goes. They can pull a huge amount of weight, compared to their size. Our old Shetland pony, Red, was so old when we acquired her that the vet couldn't even tell her age from her teeth — he said she was "well over 25" ...the equivalent to an 85-year-old-PLUS human. But old Red spent her winters outdoors, dug down through snow to nibble stubble grass, and actually swam in a pond in the summer to eat pond plants. Her biggest health problem was *obesity*.

Pony, "Red" — cold and snow doesn't faze her.

The third trait — that natural frustration at being small — is a little harder to deal with. Shetlands get downright angry at bigger horses, and will try to bully and badger them to show their psychic-superiority. Bigger horses don't like this, understandably, and — boom! — the fight is on. If there aren't any bigger horses for a Shetland to take out its frustration upon, the pony will do the same for cattle, sheep, and ...in a pinch... you, too. We've never seen a Shetland that was mean to little kids though — we suspect that's because if they menaced children, they didn't make it beyond the place they were born. This doesn't mean there aren't kid-hating Shetlands!

Welsh ponies are a little taller, about 42-46 inches at the shoulder. A more-or-less purebred Welsh will be completely black, without even a speckle of white in its coat or on its face or legs. Welsh ponies, by and large, have a more mellow temperament than Shetlands. The price of this agreeability, though, is that they are not such "easy-keepers" as Shetlands, and will require good hay and feed to keep them in shape. These ponies also can carry a "small adult" — someone up to about 130 pounds or so.

A pair of Haflingers at work at Hulston Mill, Missouri, 1999.
The cart is homemade, too.

More recently, individuals have imported a wide array of other small horses and ponies from Europe — these include Norwegian Fjords and Haflingers. There has also been a development of a "mini" breed. Fjords and Haflingers are heavy-weight small horses, very stylish, and ideal for working and pulling. These are about the size of Welsh ponies and perhaps even a little taller, heavily muscled so that they look like pony-size work horses — which is exactly what they are. Personality is generally pretty good.

The minis are a fairly new development — crosses of true miniature horses (about the size of a large dog) and Shetland-type animals. There is a tendency to breed for "gaited" animals (ones that move with a rolling motion rather than a choppy clopping), and for flashy colors. These are attractive traits, but the tendency today is to ignore the more valuable qualities of endurance, hardiness, and easy-going temperament in favor of the more dramatic and visual traits. Minis get tubby very easily, can have other health concerns related to their size and rather nervous temperament, but can live quite nicely in a big backyard. These days, before acquiring a "fancy" pony, we'd want to see it working in harness and how it behaved around children — just for safety's sake.

Working Ponies?

Okay. Let's start by saying that we like horses and ponies, have owned both continuously for nearly 15 years, and realize there is something "special" in the relationship between human and horse or pony.

These animals, and specifically ponies, can do serious work on a small farm — from plowing a garden to cultivating a field, can haul hay in a pony-sized wagon, pull kids around the neighborhood, and provide a REAL backup system in case gasoline and car parts aren't available. It's relaxing and downright fun to guide a team of ponies pulling a simple wagon or cart around the backroads; it will get you involved in lots of interesting conversations; and won't kick up as much dust (or noise!) as a truck zooming down a dirt road. There is a lot to be said for the benefits of pony-power.

A sheep ram and a pony — they always
seem to pair up and stick together.
(Photo credit: Justin Evangelista)

We also know that a tractor will not wake up in a foul mood and try to bite you. A tractor, even the "garden" variety, doesn't need to be harnessed — you just turn the key or push a button and it "goes." A tractor doesn't need daily attention, deworming, or year-around feeding — you only "feed" (gas or diesel) the tractor when you use it. A tractor will not break out through a weak point in your fence, and eat the neighbor's rare flowers. There is a lot to be said for the benefits of tractor-power.

Owning a pony or horse is really not a necessity on a homestead. Unless you work continuously with your pony, it will not save you any money — it will cost you, day-in-and day-out, just to stand around in the barnyard looking dour. This is the point where you get to decide if the ambiance, romance, emotional, and financial commitment outweighs the general nuisance-value of pony ownership.

With our usual learn-by-making-mistakes philosophy, we've stuck with the ponies anyway. Part of this is out of sheer cussedness — once or twice we've ridden or been pulled by ponies when the cars were all dead — and there just might be some kind of emergency (fat chance) where we must get out to the highway over hill-and-dale where cars won't go. And part of this is because horses and ponies have been a part of human history for millennia... something in the genes, we guess. So, our current reason for keeping these worthless hayburners is twofold: part practical, part idealism... maybe weighted heavily to idealism.

My Happy Pony Story

Sweet and gentle "Prince."
(Photo credit: Justin Evangelista)

Anita: Well, you'd think I would know better.

Prince, a sweet and gentle 10-year-old red Shetland with a big white blaze on his face, had stood around the barnyard chowing down free hay all winter. As usual, he had gained weight. One early spring afternoon, I looked at the four-legged blob and decided he needed a good workout — I'd have him haul a load of wood from the back field up to the house. That was probably my first mistake.

The second mistake was that I thought I'd just toss the new harness on him, hook him up to the little one-pony cart, and zoom out to the woods. This was a mistake because the harness had never been on this pony, and needed considerable adjustment. He'd never pulled that particular cart either.

The third mistake was rushing to do all this before the BIG STORM that was moving in broke and gushed all over the place. The wind was whipping up, trees swaying, dark clouds zooming overhead, distant lightning flashing and grumbling.

Third mistake's the charm, right?

Twenty minutes later, the harness is fastened in place. Prince is dancing nervously, yanking on the lead rope that attaches him to the wood fence. Every movement near his blindered-face makes him shy back, frantically trying to LOOK LOOK LOOK at this flapping terror that has seized him.

Speaking softly, sometimes singing (between anxious glances at the darkening sky), I manage to keep Prince from going completely nuts. He leads, skittering, across the front yard to the pony cart. All the dogs bark crazily at him, as if they have never seen this pony before. Rain begins to spatter around us.

A little teeny voice, somewhere deep in my head, says "Put the horse away and go inside before you both get fried by lightning." I ignore it. I know what I'm doing.

Prince spots the cart, struggles backward and nearly pulls the lead out of my hands in his terror. I fight masterfully, my innate human superiority winning the battle (plus the fact that I had total control of his head, thanks to the bridle). Now, standing stiffly, twitching and shivering, Prince lets me move the cart into position. I recite poetry as I attach cart straps into place — the rhythmic sounds of poems and songs seem to calm horses. Prince lets me get everything in place.

Rain is now coming down in big splats all around us. The sheep and goats have made a beeline for the barn, and are peering out at this strange turn of events in the front yard. Lightning crashes nearby. It is very loud.

Taking the lead rope firmly in hand, I carefully "clk clk," and Prince steps forward. He feels the tug of the cart — and adjusts! I breathe a slow sigh of relief...

...just a moment too soon.

One cartwheel catches on a little stone sticking up from the ground... the cart pulls obliquely... Prince throws his head up, panicking at the sudden twist against his side.

He surges forward, throwing his full weight against the terror behind him. I hold the lead, being dragged, as the cart slams into my leg.

Suddenly, Prince turns — and, horrors, the entire bridle flies off his head! He is out of control!

He throws himself forward, to the side, and down he goes, cart still attached! The cart flies over onto its side, almost overturns — for an instant, Prince is on his back, sharp hooves plunging at the air. He's so terrified, his eyes wide and white, that he sees nothing, hears nothing — only the need to throw off this monster that is dragging at him!

The cart shifts back to its side, pulling Prince along. He's on his side, kicking frantically. One hoof makes contact with the cart — wood splinters fly. Abruptly, Prince leaps to his feet, harness slipping around his abdomen, curling around his flying hooves, a thousand flat-nylon snakes threatening him even more.

He gives an excellent impression of a snorting, leaping, rodeo bronco all the way across the front yard.

The harness falls off. In pieces.

Minutes later, Prince is quietly snuffling up grass. I walk up to him, expecting the worst. He acts as if nothing had happened. It's pouring now, and thunder crashes every few seconds. I put the lead around his neck, directing him unresisting back into the barnyard, and he moseys into the barn with the other critters.

Nobody hurt, including Prince. The cart has one little part broken — easily fixed — the pieces seem to have gone into earth orbit; they are nowhere to be found. The storm passes without incident.

The happy part? Two days later, we try again — and Prince is the perfect gentleman.

Let that be a lesson to him!

Chapter Nineteen
So You Want Bees

Nick: This is how we got started with bees:
Anita came rushing excited into my work room one May afternoon.

"Guess what?" she said with great enthusiasm.

"What?" I asked cautiously. I knew that tone.

"We're getting bees."

"What?"

"You know, bees. Buzz, buzz, buzz."

I put my head down on my desk, and closed my eyes. Anita was off on another tear. This time, though, my life was over for sure. Bees, for crying out loud. Bees! Why not just put a bullet through my brain, and get it over with?

"Why?" was the only thing I could think of saying. Such farm-related conversations were not new to me: "Let's try *this* now!" Aggg!.

All I could see ahead of me was a contorted, bee-sting bloated body moldering on the hillside. *My* contorted, bee-sting bloated body, of course.

"It was Joan Haller's idea," Anita explained. The lady in question was a close friend of my wife at the time.

"I didn't know she hated me, and wanted to see me dead."

"She doesn't hate you. It's just that her husband has all the bee suit gear and the hive boxes. Everything. He kept bees for ages."

"Well, if he's so experienced, why bring me into the deal?"

"That's the problem. He took care of bees for so many years, he's burned out on it. He just doesn't want to anymore. But they'd both like to have fresh honey again."

"So, I have to die for their selfish desires?"

"They're letting us use all their equipment in exchange for part of the honey we collect."

"You mean, what I, Nick Evangelista, collect, don't you?" I interrupted.

Anita continued undaunted.

"They'll even pay for the bees for the hive. It's a perfect arrangement."

"Perfect for who... whom? Do I look like I'm contemplating suicide?"

"I couldn't say no."

I shook my head.

"I'll be glad to say no. See. No, no, no, no, no. And no!"

"We got sheep, didn't we? That turned out okay, didn't it?"

"Sheep run away from you. They don't dive bomb you, and pump your body full of toxins until you go away and die. The term is killer *bees*. Ever hear of killer *sheep?*"

Anita gave me her *How can you pass up such a good thing?* look.

"How can you pass up on such a good thing?" she said.

"What's so good about the possibility of ten thousand tiny bee stingers being embedded in my face? I'm not ready to go to heaven with a puffy complexion."

"What makes you think you're going to heaven?"

I ignored the editorial.

"You know, your 'good' threshold is somewhat less developed than mine."

"Oh, don't worry so much about being stung. That's what the bee uniform is for. It protects you."

"Come on, I'm not completely bereft of brain cells. Every time you see something about bees on television — like on PBS — the bee guys talk about being stung. 'Yah,' they say, 'they sting me all the time. But I don't feel it anymore.' Then, they laugh like bees have made a hive inside their skulls. Hey, call me quirky, but I don't want to be drilled by bees. I don't even like being vaccinated."

"I'm sure it's not as bad as all that."

"That's what you said when I had to clean out the septic tank by hand."

"You lived."

"But I didn't want to. I smelled like an outhouse for a year!"

"Only a year?"

"Listen, if you think this is such a great idea, you take care of the bees."

"You know I'm allergic to bee stings."

"Great! Another reason to invite bees onto our property. Talk about death wishes. Why don't we just hire an ax murderer to come to our house to chop firewood for us? He can do us in all at once. Why drag it out with tiny, lethal insect jabs?"

Anita hit me with her stock attack.

"Don't you want to grow as a person?"

I shrugged.

"Sure, I want to grow as a person. But the key word here is *grow*. Not *swell up*."

"What would you say if I told you the bees are already on order?"

"I'd say, I'm surprised you don't have them waiting out on the front porch."

Anita frowned.

"You think bee stings are painful — keep it up, funny boy."

I closed my eyes, and sighed.

"I don't know anything about bees. I don't want to know anything about bees. I have no interest in bees."

"You hate bees! What an awful attitude. Bees are one of Nature's wonders."

"Hey, I don't hate bees. I think bees are great. I think bees should have their own weekly television series. On *PBS*. I just don't want to raise livestock that's better armed than I am."

Silence.

Suddenly, my life seemed incredibly ponderous.

"Do we have to do this?" I asked. "I mean, is it a requirement of my life that I become a beekeeper?"

My wife bowed her head.

"No. Not if you don't want to."

I beamed.

"Really?"

Anita gave me a long, wrong-answer stare. Then she let me have it with her final salvo right in the chops: *GUILT*.

"All right. I'll tell Joan to cancel the order. Then, no one will have fresh honey. Not the Hallers, not you, not me, not our children...."

She had me. I couldn't take it anymore. I was beaten. I had to give in now or hear forever how my unpleasant selfish attitude was killing the masses of India, depriving poor Tiny Tim of his Christmas goose, and probably rending apart the very fabric of the Universe.

"Okay, okay, okay, okay, okay!"

"Okay what?"

I bit my lip.

"I know I'm going to regret this, but let's get those bees in here."

Anita smiled.

"You're sure now?"

"Oh, yes," I said. "I love bees."

"I wouldn't want you to do anything you felt wrong about."

"Okay."

"They'll be here tomorrow."

I took a deep breath.

"I can hardly wait to start growing as a person."

✹✹✹✹✹✹

Our bees were ordered from Sears.

Talk about surrealism.

Kenmore bees?

The bees — Italian bees, to be specific — were shipped to us via the postal system from Georgia. Somehow it doesn't seem right having bees delivered by the mailman, but I guess it's better than having them just swoop down out of the sky on you.

Of course, they arrived long before I was ready for them psychologically. Long, long, long.

The colony came in a shipping box with wire screens on the sides. The low, droning buzz emanating energetically from inside the container suggested the bees were not happy. They definitely arrived too soon to my way of thinking. I could have waited another two or three or four years. Maybe five.

I peered down uneasily at the box.

"Those little guys sound real upset," I observed.

Anita studied the information sheet that arrived with the bees.

"It says right here that the bees will be tired and hungry after their long trip, and that we should feed them. That's supposed to put them in better spirits."

"Then they won't want to kill us?"

"Let's hope."

"So what should we feed them?" I asked. "How about something nice and heavy? Pork chops, mashed potatoes with gravy, maybe a chocolate mousse for dessert? That should slow them down some."

"The instructions say a sugar water syrup brushed onto the container screen will be adequate."

We followed the tip. I mixed up a batch of sweet, viscous guck, and brushed it onto the wire with a basting brush. The bees devoured it with buggish enthusiasm, and before long, they calmed down.

At least they sounded better.

"What's next?" I inquired.

"They need to be moved to the brood chamber — the big bee box."

I frowned.

"That's what I was afraid of. I guess that's my job, huh?"

"You bet, bee boy."

"So how do I go about putting bees in the brood box? I take it it's a little more complicated than saying, 'Get in there, bees.'"

"More than likely."

"Do we saddle up the horse, and have a big bee drive? Or do I just grab up handfuls of bees, and stuff them into the hive? You know, to show them who's in charge."

Anita gave me a sidelong glance.

"I can see you've been studying. You'll do fine."

"I'm only joking."

"Why don't I go get that book we bought on beekeeping. It should have enough information on handling bees to keep you from hurting them."

"*Me* hurt *them?*"

"Just wait."

"*Me* hurt *them?*"

"Wait."

"Okay, I'll wait, I'll wait!"

Anita went to her work room, and returned with our newly purchased bee manual.

"So, that's a bee," I said, pointing at the cover photo.

Anita ignored me.

"Let's see what the book says," she suggested.

I shook my head.

"I'm not ready for this."

Anita patted my hand.

"You'll do just fine."

"You say."

"You will." She paused. "Anyway, it says right here you have a few more hours to prepare yourself."

"Why's that?"

"It is suggested that the bees be transferred to their box at dusk. Their instinct is to normally head for shelter as the sun goes down, and they'll take more readily to being installed into the hive then."

"Great! A stay of execution."

Anita smiled.

"Just remember it's only a postponement. You haven't been pardoned."

"I know, I know."

✖✖✖✖✖✖

Dressed in my heavy, white bee suit, thickly ponderous rubber gloves, and tightly veiled beekeeper pith helmet, I trudged slowly up the hillside toward the hive box. We'd placed it as far away from our house as we could get it and still be on our own property. I carried the bee transport cage gingerly in both hands. I felt like I was doing bomb squad duty. UXB: unexploded bees.

The insects hummed noncommittally.

"I hate this."

"I'll be right behind you," Anita had said to me as I was leaving.

"Yah, a thousand feet right behind me," I'd replied. "I'm comforted."

"Now, you're sure you know what to do?"

"Of course. When I'm stung, I scream, contort, and fall down."

"Very, very funny."

When I reached the hive box, I set the bees down lightly on the ground. My heart was thumping. Sweat poured down my face. I could almost hear the ticking bomb I had to defuse.

"Please be nice, bees," I pleaded. "I like you."

I'd gone over and over the transferring process, and I was pretty sure I knew how to handle our new pets.

I removed the lid from the hive box, and looked inside. The brood chamber was all set to go. I'd already set up foundation wax in frames to receive the bees' first honey. A feeder jar, filled with sugar water to help the insects through their first days in their new home, sat in one corner.

I stared at the bees for a long, long time.

"Okay," I said to myself, "I guess I can't put this off any longer."

I pried open the lid on the top of the transport cage. The bees didn't come swarming out in a killer frenzy. They just sat there. A good sign.

Then, my hands shaking, I began dumping thousands of bees into the hive. The sobering quality of being in such close proximity to so many potentially pain-creating insects was not lost on me. As I jiggled the cage, they fell in thick, clinging clumps, like damp balls of cracker jacks, onto the floor of the box. To my surprise, they stayed where they landed.

When the cage was emptied of bees, I set the small box containing the queen and her attendants in the hive. Our bee book had cautioned not to open the queen box but to allow the workers to eat through the candy plugs at each end, and let her out themselves. That way, they would have time to get used to her, and not execute her as an intruder.

Ah!

That done, I quickly replaced the lid on the hive, and made sure all openings were sealed tightly. In three or four days, when the bees had accepted the box as home, they could be set free to start up their new life on our farm.

Everything was as it should be.

The bees were battened down.

I breathed a sigh of relief.

The ticking had stopped.

The bomb was defused.

I'd faced the bee horde and survived.

❊❊❊❊❊❊

"How'd it go?" Anita asked me when I returned to the house.

I shrugged, pulling off my beekeeper coat.

"No big deal."

"Really?"

"In fact," I lied, "it was kind of fun."

Chapter Twenty Jurassic Barnyard or, How We Learned to Live With Chickens

We knew an old guy who raised chickens for fifty years. His only advice was: "Don't let them things near your eyes."

Progressive paleontologists, dinosaur scientists, think birds are direct descendants of dinosaurs. It has something to do with wishbones. We think that's what it is. Now, if this really is so, then chickens are, in essence, dinosaurs.

We can buy that. Watching two roosters go at it in the barnyard, spurred feet slashing and clawing, or a hen, neck outstretched, running down a bug and picking it out of the air like a magician pulling a coin out of someone's ear, you kind of get the idea it's a good thing God decided to shrink dinosaurs to a manageable size. A thirty-foot chicken would be a difficult member of the web of life to deal with in a pleasant manner.

There's definitely something primordial in chicken personalities, a simple savage, kill-or-be-killed quality. Not very endearing. We could see them flapping around in dinosaur times, the Mesozoic Era, pecking holes in a poor stegosaurus until it flopped over in an exhausted heap. Leghornasaurus. Brahmadon. Cluckatops.

Dinosaurs?
(Photo credit: Justin Evangelista)

✖ ✖ ✖ ✖ ✖ ✖

Nick: Anita and I have raised chickens for years. Rhode Island Reds, Japanese Silkies, Bearded Polish, Brahmas, Anconas, Black Minorcas, Turkens, Cochins, Cornish, Leghorns, Bantams — a real collection. I wanted to call this chapter "Satan's Beaked Buddies." But Anita said, "Sheesh. Get real. They're *nobody's* buddy." Okay, okay! So, we settled on the dinosaur theme.

✖ ✖ ✖ ✖ ✖ ✖

Basically, chickens are mean-tempered, greedy monsters. And very dumb, underneath those pretty feathers. Like we said, we raise chickens. But we're not what you would call chicken *fanciers*.

Admittedly, at first glance, you wouldn't necessarily give chickens a *thumbs down*. Watching them strut and peck around a farm for a bit, they seem about as peaceful, wholesome, and benign as any other kind of livestock. A farm isn't a farm without chickens. Right? But, you live with them, day in and day out, their true Jurassic nature begins to surface. Specifically?

You think buzzards are bad, or crows, or owls when it comes to disagreeable personalities? Chickens are rabid garbage bins for anything they can fit into their beaks. This can be good if you want to get rid of some grossly spoiled refrigerator food, or some fat worms freshly plucked from your tomato patch.

A food-shop-owning in-law wanted to demonstrate his attitude toward a particular brand of imported cheese. He gave us a couple pounds for the hens — provided we took pictures of whatever the chickens did with it, to send to his supplier. See that photo with the chickens attacking a hunk of something? The in-law saw the pictures, laughed until he choked, was red in the face, and too weak to sit upright. He taped them all over his office desk. We don't think the supplier ever got to see one.

Chickens won't necessarily stop at that. They'll gladly gobble down each other, dead or alive. One shows a bit of psychological weakness, or gets a little down in the beak health-wise, and whamo! There's a meal just waiting to happen. Chickens, simply put, are cannibals of the worst sort. Man-munching ancient Aztecs had nothing on chickens.

Even cute, little, fuzzy peeping chick-types — oh, they're so cute! — will sometimes peck each other to bloody bits with gusto at the slightest provocation. Of course, don't think you're outside their purview when it comes to food. They might not be able to eat you, but that won't keep them from trying.

Anita: My older brother, Bill, has a childhood memory from nearly 60-years-ago. He remembered being a toddler and wandering into someone's chicken pen. To his pint-sized self, the hens were as big as giant *turkeys* — nearly as big as he was. The enormous rooster marched up to him, took one meaty peck out of his face — and set off a hen feeding frenzy... that consisted of Bill! Suddenly, he was awash in a sea of feathers, all intent on getting a nice bite out of the tender pale thing in the knickers. Bill swung wildly, his little eyes clamped tightly shut against the attack. He felt his bunched fists slam satisfyingly into writhing feathered bodies, heard the intent buc-buc sound hens make when tasting something *good*, and gave his all to the eternal battle: man versus velociraptor. Well, toddler versus hen, anyway. Some adult raced to his aid, and yanked him from the pen — bloodied, but not bowed.

Bill just never liked *turkeys* after that. Go figure.

So, whatever you do, don't let them near your eyes. Ever see the movie *The Birds*? Think of that, only with chickens.

❈ ❈ ❈ ❈ ❈ ❈

Chickens chowing cheese.

As owners of chickens, you are faced with two possible approaches to raising them: you can allow them to be free range birds (that is, they go where they want to go), or you can keep them in pens or cages.

With the latter method, you can keep them pretty much under control, but you have to feed them all the time, and that costs money or requires committing some land to growing chicken food. Also, they tend to be more healthy and robust as free rangers.

On the other hand, when you go with free rangers, you have healthy birds that may generate all sorts of problems. Like they'll hide their eggs, which you'll only find a few years later. (These may explode when you touch them, so be careful! Believe us, you don't want to know what they smell like.) Or maybe the birds will end up being eaten by dogs or raccoons or skunks, which seems to be the lot of many free range chickens — that's an expense, too. Sometimes, it seems like they go out of their way to have this happen.

Anyway, take your pick.

❋❋❋❋❋❋

Got any other horror stories? You ask.

Sure, how's this?

How can we put this delicately? Chickens have pretty poor elimination practices. For Shakespeare, all the world was a stage. For chickens, all the world is a toilet. One of their most cherished activities is relieving themselves anywhere you'll be walking regularly.

They have mental maps, much in the manner of homing pigeons and swallows. It must be their special task in nature — distributing their own brand of plant enhancing fertilizer. Unfortunately, you might not think so highly of this practice the first time you track their offering on the heel of your boot across your nice, clean living room carpet... probably a white carpet.

What the heck is that? You'll begin, squinting at the unfamiliar substance. Then, as the truth filters in, your opinion of chickens will become R-rated (for *adult language*).

Other favorite chicken elimination areas include the following locations: under your car (especially if you do your own car repair and have to spend time sliding around under it. Repeat after me: *What's that on the back of my head?*); on feed hay bales for other livestock (a nice breeding ground for disease); in other animals' feeders and water bowls (more disease-spreading); on other animals (when you get a hen or rooster that decides to roost at night up in the barn rafters); and on you (for the same reason).

This, of course, is a problem only when they are allowed to roam around on their own.

✕✕✕✕✕✕

Too bad they don't have obedience schools for chickens. We'd enroll ours. Well, maybe they do: they're called restaurants.

✕✕✕✕✕✕

One time, we read in a farm magazine that the best way to keep bugs out of the garden was to put chickens in the garden with the bugs. We tried this.

Well, it sort of worked. The chickens did keep bugs out of our garden. But, as it turned out, they also kept food out of our garden. The chickens especially liked to poke holes in our pumpkins, tomatoes, and squash, which pretty much ruined them, to our way of thinking.

We decided to put an end to this experiment. Unfortunately, we'd created an army of Frankenchicks. Did they think they were done? Definitely not! Once the door was thrown open, they kept up their decimating ways with an energetic single-mindedness bordering on satanic. There was plenty for them to eat elsewhere. But now they *had* to eat our growing foods. They were obsessive about this, *compelled*. Not wanting them in the garden equaled their desire to be nowhere but the garden, no other place to go on this great, wide planet. It was spooky.

We tried feeding them vast quantities of grain to distract them. But this didn't even slow them down. They just got fatter. And more insistent.

After a long, long period of chasing chickens (which included yelling *adult language* and throwing rocks), we finally built a nice woven-wire fence, which the chickens then flew over. We clipped their wings, but, somehow they still got in. We began to suspect they were simply materializing in the garden (you start to get some pretty dumb ideas when you're really frustrated).

In the end, the only cure was to build a huge pen and chicken house for the chickens. That meant no more free range, of course; but the garden was ours again. Sometimes you have to compromise with reality.

❋❋❋❋❋❋

Nick: This is my most memorable chicken story:

It happened one morning when I was out milking goats in our barn. I'd already gotten close to two gallons of milk, keeping it in a nice big milk bucket up on a shelf secured to our milk stand (where it was safe from dirt and goat behavior). I was working on my last goat udder for the morning when, suddenly, the bucket filled with milk came crashing down square on my head. I never saw it coming. Milk drenching me, I slowly looked upward to observe the chicken that had decided to perch on the shelf. The chicken cocked its head, looking at me with one red, staring eye. I, of course, was not happy.

Chickens were not allowed in the milking area after that. *You learn.*

❌❌❌❌❌❌

More than ever, we think that dinosaur/bird theory is probably the correct notion. You couldn't develop chicken personalities even in a dozen centuries. You'd need them getting their start in the teeming wilds of some Jurassic forest.

You want some really scary dinosaur behavior for your next dinosaur movie, Mr. Spielberg? Come out to our farm for a few days, and watch the chickens.

❌❌❌❌❌❌

Wait a minute, you say, there must be something good about chickens. Otherwise, who would want to keep them?

Well, yes, there are nice things about chickens. One: they roast up nicely at 350 degrees. Two: eggs. And, three: they look pretty mounted and stuffed.

Eggs, of course, are the easiest form of chickens to deal with. We sometimes refer to them as *chicken starter kits*. They are quiet, they don't raid gardens, and they don't poop.

There are, it should be noted, people who love to raise chickens. But they have drugs now that can suppress such urges.

Chapter Twenty One
The Poisonous Snake

Nick: Living in the country can be full of surprises. It was a quiet summer afternoon when the phone rang innocently. I answered it without a second thought.

"Hello."

"Nick?" It was our neighbor down the road, Lexie Kimbrough. Her voice was strained.

"What's up?" I asked.

She paused, as if to gather in the full feeling of what she wanted to tell me.

"There's a copperhead down in my barn. And J.L. isn't here. He's been out bailing hay since early this morning." J.L. was Lexie's husband. "Could you help me with it?"

A copperhead. A poisonous snake! We'd seen all kinds of snakes since we arrived in the Ozarks: black snakes, king snakes, hog-nosed snakes, garter snakes, and worm snakes. Some inside our house, living in our walls. But we'd never met a poisonous snake before in person. People had told us tales of copperhead encounters — including the parts about limbs ballooning to triple size, gangrene, and amputations — but we'd been spared the pleasure up to now.

The Kimbroughs were friends. They'd done us countless favors. I couldn't say no.

"I'll be right over," I said. I hung up the phone.

"What's up?" Anita asked.

"Lexie's got a copperhead in her barn, and she wants me to catch it for her."

"Where's J.L.?"

"He's out baling hay. I have to go."

Anita nodded slowly. "This is dangerous, you know."

"You're telling me! I don't have much of a choice, though. Lexie was pretty shaken. You can't have poisonous snakes hopping around your barn."

"Slithering. Well, be careful."

"Like I'm not petrified all ready. Do I look pale?"

"No more than usual."

"Thanks." I sighed. "Well, it's been nice knowing you."

"You be careful, you idiot."

"I know: if you touch it with your hands, wash afterwards. You don't know where it's been."

"Don't touch it at all if you can help it!!"

"Only joking."

I pushed open the front door.

"See you."

"Wear your gloves!" Anita called after me.

"Got 'em."

I was pretty sure this was not going to be fun time. I don't much like snakes, but poisonous ones are definitely on my "don't invite" list.

❈❈❈❈❈❈

Lexie Kimbrough was standing in the doorway to her barn when I arrived. She looked relieved when she saw me. She was holding a shotgun.

"I'm sorry to have you come down here like this," she said.

"It's okay," I said. "What's going on?"

Lexie leaned the shotgun against the wall.

"When I first saw the snake, I was going to shoot it. But there's all this farm machinery in here. It would have made a real mess. I don't think J.L. would have been happy with me putting holes in his tractor."

"Probably not," I agreed. Shooting willy-nilly in the barn was definitely a no-no — that little ricochet problem.

I looked around.

"So where's the copperhead?"

Lexie pointed.

"There it is."

I squinted. I could just barely make it out in the shadows, the snake, coiled up in a large glass jar, staring defiantly at us. I could just imagine Lexie blasting the jar, sending bits of glass and snake and shotgun pellets flying into every corner of the barn. "Terminator III : Farm Fun."

"What's it doing in a jar?" I asked.

Lexie shook her head.

"It was just there when I came out to get some calf feed."

"Maybe it was just looking for a safe place to take a nap or something," I suggested.

"Well, what do you want to do?" Lexie asked.

What I wanted to do was go home, but I didn't say that, of course.

I studied the situation. My first thought was that I didn't want to get near the snake with any part of my body.

A moment later, I had a plan.

"Do you have a big bucket?"

"Why?"

"Well, I was thinking, that jar is just sitting there on the edge of that table. If I can knock it off with something into a bucket, we can throw some kind of lid on top, and trap it inside."

Lexie brightened.

"I have just the bucket in the house. It's one of those big white plastic ones. And it has a lid. I'll go get it."

Now, we were getting some place!

Lexie headed off to the house.

I watched the snake, hoping it wouldn't try to take off. It didn't move, though. It just kept staring at me with those cold, emotionless snake eyes. I thought about grabbing the jar, and dropping it into the bucket, but I didn't know how fast copperheads could move. I didn't want to find out either.

Then, I noticed a rake with a nice, long handle in the corner. That would do for tipping the jar, I decided.

Finally, after what seemed like a year or two, Lexie returned with the bucket.

"Great," I said. "That's perfect."

"Has it moved?" Lexie asked.

"Not an inch."

"It looks mean," she added.

Great, I thought. Mean and poisonous.

I took the bucket, and cautiously positioned it right beneath the jar. I took everything into consideration: the height of the fall, the angle, everything. I was careful. This was going to work.

Then I stepped back, and hooked the rake on the jar, and pulled.

The rest seemed to happen in slow motion:

The jar tipped, and fell. Instead of dropping into the bucket, though, it hit the bucket's edge, and bounced into the air. I watched, horrified. The jar landed at my feet, and the snake came slipping out. Lexie screamed, disappearing out the barn door. I jumped back, and brought the rake down hard on the copperhead, who then bounced like a rubber ball high into the air, and smacked me right in the face.

Throwing the rake away, I almost made a new barn door, as I made my escape.

Chapter Twenty One
The Poisonous Snake

199

When thought returned, I went back to the barn to see if there was any sign of the snake.

I found the copperhead laying where I'd left it. It looked like it was dead. I picked up my discarded rake, and prodded it a couple times. If it wasn't dead, it was sure having one heck of a sound sleep.

Lexie peered into the barn.

"Where's the snake? Did it get away?"

I pointed.

"It's right here," I said. "I think it's dead now. I must have killed it when I hit it with the rake."

"It's not squirming."

I scratched my head.

"That's funny. They don't usually die without some kind of wiggling. Like when they get run over in the road by a car."

I prodded the snake again. It seemed unusually limp and rubbery. I touched it with my finger. It was kind of soft.

"You know," Lexie suggested, "I think that snake has been dead for a long time."

I nodded.

"So, basically, I just killed a dead snake."

"I think so," Lexie Kimbrough agreed.

❆❆❆❆❆❆

I found out later that evening that Lexie's husband J.L. had killed the snake out in the field while he was baling hay, took it to the barn to dispose of it, and then just forgot about it.

Surprise!

Section Three
Wrapping It Up

Chapter Twenty Two
Country Roads:
The Reality of Abandoned Farms

The back roads of the country are littered with empty, deserted farmhouses, forgotten and falling down, overgrown, silent testaments to the arbitrary harshness of the country existence. It's easy to overlook them, to ignore them, to dismiss them with the merest thought or comment. They're such a part of the scenery.

Yet, these ruined places have a message for us, and their message is a clear one. They remind anyone who lives in rural America that this particular world can't be taken for granted, that farm life, often unfriendly, even violent, and most certainly changeable, requires constant vigilance, planning, and, above all, fortitude for personal survival.

It's a sobering thought that these falling down collections of rotting wood and broken glass, amid the weeds, brambles, and knee-high grass, were once home to folks probably not much different than one's self.

They nurtured their hopes and dreams and plans of future work, a sense of prosperity, and a notion of stability and continuity in their lives. In the Ozarks, many of them planted golden jonquil bulbs around their front door — bulbs that send up springtime shoots, and bloom sunshine yellow against a sea of green.

You can almost see those people going about their daily chores: feeding the pigs and cows and chickens, planting gardens, mending fences, the stuff of which farm days are made.

So where did these people go? Where did their dreams disappear to? What sent them spiraling down to disaster and abandonment? When does a shout of assurance become a hollow cry of enough is enough?

We sometimes look at our own farm, and wonder how solid it really is. We plan for the future, too.

The jonquils keep arriving each spring, sometimes arising around bare foundation stones, deep in a stretch of oak woods.

It makes you think.

Chapter Twenty Three
Far Out in the Boonies:
Good Idea?

So, you've been living in the middle of some big city. Your nearest neighbor is fifteen or twenty feet away from you at any given point in time — on either side, above, or below. Feeling like a caged animal, you dream of living in the country, with its wide open spaces, its quiet, its sense of laid back solitude. You can't wait to be there.

This is your dream. But is it necessarily a good idea? You'd better think about it a bit before you leap.

Too far out — or not far enough?
(Photo credit: Justin Evangelista)

Country Living is Risky Business

206

Why?

Answer: Because being alone, out in the middle of nowhere, has its down side, too. While we've described some of the effects of this situation through our own *bad* experiences, it needs to be repeated. We remember that we had some pretty dead-wrong thoughts about rural life before we actually slammed into it. Unless you've actually spent a lot of time alone in the past, being out away from everything can drive you nuts.

1. It can hit your paranoia button. You can start imagining all kinds of nutty things on a dark summer night. What's this sound? What's that on the roof? Did you hear something strange out in the barn? Then, there was that news report about the loonie who just escaped from the mental hospital not ten miles from where you live.

2. Without your normal stimuli around you, you can really lose your focus, getting nothing done a lot of the time.

3. You'd better have a real sense of self-reliance, because there will be times when you, and you alone, will be there to take care of emergencies, mechanical breakdowns, whatever. If the nearest town is twenty miles away, you're in charge, buddy.

4. Occasional isolation can be fun, but try it for days on end. You might be snowbound on your property for a month. Maybe there's an ice storm, and the roads are too slick to even crawl on, much less drive on. Maybe the usually dry riverbed you have to drive through to get to town, has ten-feet-deep flashflood water roaring through its course, and the only way you'll get across is with an ark. Maybe your only transportation vehicle is broken, and you just don't have the bucks to get it fixed right now. You are there, and you are staying there. Somehow, enforced isolation ends up being much worse than voluntary exile. It seems that having a choice in the matter makes a big difference.

5. Another thing: If you're fine with living out in nowhere land, but your spouse isn't, this can lead to real relationship problems. It's a fact that more than one couple who moved to the country has ended up divorcing. The last two husband-and-wife teams who owned our farm before we did, broke up from the strain of one person not making the transition from city to country life. This is a reality.

6. Being far away from towns can remove you from financial possibilities — if you happen to be interested in that sort of thing. If you can work out of your isolated location, that's fine. But, if you can't, you still have to pay your bills.

7. If entertainment is important to you — movies, plays, fine restaurants, museums — you will find none of these in the country. If you are not enthralled with the country, and don't find just being there is a reward in itself; if you are totally without the ability to find ways to amuse yourself; if you have a low boredom threshold — then forget moving to the country. You will not be able to handle it.

8. If you're telling your city friends that living in the country will be just like living in the city — only with fewer people around, drop your plans to move right this minute. You have the wrong mindset. You will be back in the city before you know what has hit you.

9. If you think your transition from the city to the country — no matter the already perceived differences — will be quick and painless, you might be insane.

10. Finally, if you think you can live way out in the middle of nowhere, pushing away any neighbors you might have as though you were a kingdom and a power unto yourself, think again. Cultivate your neighbors. You don't have to have them over every day for tea, just say hi and stop to "jaw" about the weather for a minute or two. They

probably don't want you over on a regular basis either. That's the way it is with country folks. But when you find yourself sitting in your car bogged down in the mud somewhere, and there's no one to help pull you out; or you need one more strong back to get that beam up for that barn you're building, well, you'll wish you knew that neighbor down the road well enough to ask him for a favor. Being far out in the country doesn't mean being anti-social.

Anyway, these are just a few thoughts about living out in the boonies. Take them or leave them as you will.

Chapter Twenty Four
Ten Good Ideas for
Country Survival

Here are some possibly helpful thoughts on keeping your life going in the country:

1. *Attitude*

Never get involved in any plan of action you absolutely hate the idea of doing — just because you think "it's what you're supposed to do when you move to the country." This can mean anything from raising a particular type of livestock to following a supposed "farm" diet. If it is not in you to do this thing, you will do it badly.

2. *Time Well Spent*

There are books that cater to a nineteenth century country lifestyle. Make candles, build your own furniture, construct fences out of timber you fell yourself, and so on. This is fine. This is nice. Is your time valuable? Don't mess with this stuff unless you can afford a hobby. Candles are cheap. If you can't afford furniture, check out the thrift shop in the town closest to you. As for fences, metal ones last longer than wood ones. Don't be quaint. Be smart. Put your time to good use.

3. *Stretched Too Thin*
Don't over extend yourself. Having too many plans all at once will only cause you to lose your focus. You will get nothing done, and frustration will set in. Or, you will do a little bit of a lot, and get nothing completely done.

4. *Public Relations*
Don't offend your country neighbors with a superior attitude. You might need their help some day. Remember, they've been smart enough to live their entire life in the country without self-destructing. Can you say the same thing?

5. *All Your Eggs in One Basket*
You will be more likely to succeed with your back-to-the-land dream if you sensibly diversify your operation. Placing your hopes on the success of a single pursuit — sheep, goats, hogs, cattle, pumpkin sales, eggs, whatever — will end up being your downfall. A bit of this and that, small-scale stuff, is where you'll make your living. You can't compete with the huge corporations these days. When you diversify, you can go after the small markets, the ones the big guys overlook or don't care about. This approach to farm marketing becomes your strength.

6. *Self-Reliance*
Country folk are among the most giving people you'll ever come across. But, when you're having problems, don't expect them to coddle you. When they help, they expect you to pull your own weight. Anything less, and you'll pretty much alienate your neighbors.

7. *Fencing*
Always make sure the fences around your property are up and doing their job. When your animals are continually

grazing on someone else's land, bad feelings can escalate quickly into something really ugly. The saying, "Good fences make for good neighbors," didn't originate out of the blue, you know.

8. *Security*

Want to lose that loving feeling about the area you've moved to? Have your house burglarized. People in the country used to leave home with all their doors unlocked, but not anymore. Criminal types have finally figured out that isolated farms don't possess much in the way of home security. It is therefore best to do what you can to minimize the danger of burglary by always being vigilant to this fact. Get a big dog. Never publicize your vacations in public. Be mindful of who you give out your address to. And find ways to make it look like you're always at home, even when you're not. Having your country home pillaged is not a very positive inducement to continuing your life in the country.

9. *Gambling*

Don't go out on a limb financially. Sure things are rarely sure things. This can be in regard to speculating in exotic livestock, or simply trying to make a killing in a conventional agricultural method. Our realtor suggested we "get into cattle" — raise two calves, sell one at a profit; put the other into the freezer "for free." He forgot to tell us the part about costly cattle pens, sturdy-loading chutes, hauling trailers, and how calves sometimes run away or die. Get all the facts before you invest.

10. *Procrastination*

We wrote about procrastination in *Blood-Lust Chickens and Renegade Sheep*, but it fits here, so we will mention it again. Timing in life is everything. You know the old saying, "Strike while the iron is hot." Getting things done moves you forward. Unnecessary waiting only bogs you down. And this is especially true in the country, where everything, everything, has its season.

Don't even ask how we found this out.

Epilogue

Chapter Twenty Five
Spitting on Elvis

And now for a *small town* story:
We bet almost everyone in the world has an Elvis story. Even the Pope probably has an Elvis story. The tabloids are full of Elvis-related tidbits. "I Saw Elvis's Ghost Eat 10,000 Marshmallows," "I've Got The King's Kidneys," and "Elvis' Underwear Saved My Life."

Elvis Presley has been more active in print since he passed into the Great Beyond than in all the years he was ambulatory put together. Most of these encounters, unfortunately, are ninny fare. At least, we used to think so.

Still, one has to admit — no matter what one personally thinks of Elvis' artistic capabilities or his present day mythology — his life has had an impact on our culture. This fact came crashing in on us a few years ago when our area of Missouri was experiencing a major drought.

In an attempt to relieve the ongoing dusty angst of the dehydrating populace, a local radio DJ hired an elderly Native American resident of the town to do a rather unrehearsed "rain dance" in the town square. The feather-bedecked old gent was provided with a brown bag, reputed to contain "spirits," to maintain his enthusiasm for the episode. A small, appreciative crowd gathered, and the DJ made the evening news reports for orchestrating the effort. We won't dwell on the "good taste/bad taste" aspect of the event. Miss Manners would doubtlessly have frowned.

After the entertainment was over, people moved off slowly, plump ladies gently fanning themselves against the stifling heat. Two young women sauntered past us, talking. One — tall, willowy, with that sunny, healthy Midwest glow — said, "That sure was dumb."

The other one agreed. "What a waste of time. Can you believe these people?" She used one hand to shade her eyes. "I'm going home right now and pray to Elvis for rain. He's never let me down yet."

Elvis?

Elvis *Presley?*

The final words we were able to catch were, "That's a good idea. I will, too. The King will talk to God and make it rain."

We couldn't believe it. These women looked otherwise normal. Well, normalish. They weren't wearing potato sacks. Their eyes were free of glaze. They weren't being led around on leashes by keepers. Yet, here they were, talking matter-of-factly about a heaven-bent relationship with the Burger King. Like, doesn't everybody ask defunct rock-and-rollers for miracles?

Maybe they do.

Some folks see the world from an odd angle.

❊❊❊❊❊❊

Nick: By the way, I once met Elvis.

It was 1968. I was nineteen-years-old at the time, and working as a printer's apprentice in the composing room of the old *Citizen-News* newspaper in Hollywood. One day, I heard they were shooting part of a movie down in the press room (where the printing presses are), and that Elvis Presley was the star. I didn't particularly care for Elvis flicks, but having a real live famous movie person nearby is always kind of exciting.

The scene they were filming was pretty straightforward. Elvis was supposed to be a worker on a newspaper. He has a fight with someone, and gets fired. After that, he goes on to great adventures elsewhere. They paid a number of the jokers in the press room $50 each to stand around in the background and look interested. To be honest, I never did see the movie. I don't even know what it was called.

Just the same, there we were, Elvis and me, in the same building at the same time. There was some talk of him coming upstairs to say hello to everyone, but no one knew for sure.

Eventually, I put the whole thing into the back of my mind and got down to work. Around 5:30, though, I needed to take a little break; so I slipped out to the stairwell at the back of the building. There was a landing, with an open window where a person could get some fresh air, and it was relatively quiet.

Now, I have to explain something here. Printers in those days were not the most cultured individuals around. They were, by and large, pretty gross. Even worse, if you worked around them long enough, you picked up their habits. Mostly filthy, bad, disgusting habits. For instance, they spit.

All right, I admit it: I acquired the spit habit. I never went so far as to add chewing tobacco to my routine — that would have been too foul — but I still spit a lot. I would spit out that window on the landing all the time. There was something uniquely satisfying about watching that long, drifting plunge, followed by a sharp, sound splat on the concrete below. And being a dumb, thoughtless kid, I rarely made sure if anyone was in the way.

Out on the stairs, I began to relax. I sat on the window ledge staring mindlessly off into the warm afternoon sky, wishing I was elsewhere. Suddenly, I was overcome by the usual urge to spit. I was going to launch a good, heavy bomb.

The saliva was there, warmed up and ready to go. But I stopped myself. This time, for some reason, I decided to look first. As I said, I didn't normally check before I spit. I don't know why I became so thoughtful (it took years of being outside teenagerhood for thinking to become a regular part of my make-up). I just did, that's all.

And when I looked down, there was Elvis Presley talking to a couple film people directly below the window. If I'd hung one out of the window, I'd have crowned the King, metaphorically speaking.

Being at a pretty goofy age, I thought Elvis should know what almost happened; so, with that giddy, bold stupidity that often sweeps over a regular person in the presence of fame, I called down to him.

"Hey, Elvis!" He looked directly up at me. "I almost spit on your head!"

"Well," he said, in that drawling, Elvis-kind-of-way of his, "I'm sure glad you didn't."

"Me too. See you later, Elvis."

"Take it easy, buddy."

I ducked back inside and returned to work.

I never saw Elvis in person again. He didn't come up to my work area.

That was it.

Elvis didn't take me out to dinner at the end of the day. He didn't give me one of his cars. He didn't even slip me a personal autograph. What can I say? The guy just left. He skipped. He hit the road.

The bum!

That's what happened. My Elvis Story. The end.

The kicker to the rain incident was that it began to rain the very next day — bamboozling the weather forecasters, startling the radio DJ (who was reduced to near-wordlessness), and making the entire local populace supremely happy.

Was it the rain dance? Locals who claimed Native American heritage nodded sagely and gave each other that look as they stood in soggy parking lots, and gazed smiling into the stormy sky.

Was it... Saint Elvis...?

Or was it simply one of those inexplicable quixotical moments in country living?

Resources

The single cheapest and most comprehensive place to find info on moving to the country, and on self-help and self-reliance principles, is your local library. Most small town libraries even have the capacity to make use of inter-library loans from around the country. If you're near a university, you can acquire "Friends of the Library" (or something similar) status for an annual payment ($25 or so) — which gives you access to their vast stacks of material, plus their capacity to search the Internet.

Internationally acclaimed science-fiction fantasy writer, Terry Pratchett, has this to say: "Everything I ever learned, I learned in the library. School taught me how to spit."

Books

There are many, many fine books that deal with some principles of country living and self-reliance; everybody finds a favorite that "resonates" with their own orientation and needs — ours are:

How to Live on Almost Nothing and Have Plenty: A Practical Introduction to Small-Scale Sufficient Country Living, by Janet Chadwick. (Knopf, New York, 1979.) This fine book has information on most of the types of systems you'd want to use on a small farm setting — livestock, gardening, and recipes. The author clearly enjoyed moving to the country, and made the most of her home!

Practical Skills: A Revival of Forgotten Crafts, Techniques and Traditions, by Gene Logsdon. (Rodale Press, Emmaus, PA, 1985.) The " Contrarian Farmer's" big-book-of-neat-stuff, just chock full of old timey information and skills. If you love hands-on work, this one is for you. Now sadly out-of-print, you might find a well-used copy at resale stores. Keep looking! It's worth it.

The Bread Book: A Natural Whole-Grain Seed-to-Loaf Approach to Real Bread, by Thom Leonard. (East-West Health Books, 17 Station Street, Brookline, MA 02146, 1990.) A slim volume that truly and clearly explains how to grow grain on a backyard scale, harvest and store it, and then convert it into the most incredible loaf of bread you have ever tasted! Even includes specifications for a home-made outdoor bread oven!

Homemade Liqueurs, by Dona and Mel Meilach. (Contemporary Books, Chicago, 1979.) Recipes for making the "fancy store-bought stuff" using less-expensive ingredients at home. Excellent guide to using up those excess fruits and berries.

Cheesemaking Made Easy, by Ricki and Robert Carroll. (Storey Communications, Pownal, VT, 1982.) Sixty clear and straightforward recipes for different types of homemade cheeses. Classic.

Putting Food By, by Ruth Hertzberg, Beatrice Vaughan, and Janet Greene. (Stephen Greene Press, Brattleboro, VT 05301, 1974.) Many reprints since this early edition.

Resources

223

Perhaps the most useful and comprehensive preserving book on the planet.

Cooking With the Sun: How to Build and Use Solar Cookers, by Beth Halacy and Dan Halacy. (Morning Sun Press, 1240 Quandt Road, Lafayette, CA 94549, 1992.) Lots of good basic information on solar applications, with directions for building and ideas for recipes.

Living Without Electricity, by Steven Scott and Kenneth Pellman. (Good Books, 3510 Philadelphia Pike, Intercourse, PA 17534, 19990.) Slim book that mostly looks at the non-electric Amish lifestyle — but, wow! Is it full of ideas for the handman/woman!

Foxfire Books, (Anchor, Doubleday Press.) The original collection from the 1970s was loaded with fascinating pictures, directions, ideas and applications for hands-on do-it-yourselfers. Thank goodness, there are new editions of this series available now — because our well-thumbed copies are falling apart! Warning: Once you start reding these, you can't stop!

And don't forget our earlier books: *Blood-Lust Chickens and Renegade Sheep: A First Timer's Guide to Country Living* (Loompanics Unlimited), *How to Live Without Electricity and Like It*, *How to Develop a Low-Cost Family Food-Storage System*, and *Backyard Meat Production, How to Grow All the Meat You Need in Your Own Backyard* (Breakout Productions), all available from Loompanics Unlimited.

Finally, thanks to y2k, a number of new and excellent works on basic self-reliance had a short run on the market in late 1999. For all around self-preparedness, these titles are excellent:

The Y2K Personal Survival Guide, by Michael Hyatt
The Millennium Bug, by Michael Hyatt
Making the Best of Basics, by James Talmadge Stevens
Don't Get Caught With Your Pantry Down, by James Talmadge Stevens
Y2K for Women, by Karen Anderson

Magazines

Times change, and so do magazines. In "the olden days," *The Mother Earth News* was THE place to go for really useful (if sometimes offbeat) information. "Mother" is still around, but she ain't the same gal she used to be. Issues 1-80 are really the primo country-living material, if you can get past the datedness of the politics!

Backhome Magazine, PO Box 370, Mountain Home, NC 28758. Good basic information on organic-ecological orientation magazines.

Backwoods Home Magazine, PO Box 712, Gold Beach, OR 97444. Practical, conservative, and hard-working pieces. Quality writing and lots of detail, excellent.

Small Farmer's Journal, PO Box 1627, Sisters, OR 97402. Aimed toward "horse-farming," with many useful pieces on the technicalities of working horses — but also general small-farm material and lots of interesting letters.

Countryside and Small Stock Journal, W11564 Hwy 64, Withee, WI 54498. Mostly reader written, lots of hands-on advice, really gives a "feel" for the mood and temperment of the small holder today.

Country Journal, PO Box 420585, Palm Coast, FL 32142. You may be able to find this one on your newsstands — it's different than the "other" *Country Journal* published by Reiman, which is loaded with pretty photographs and not much hard-core stuff. This *Country Journal* has undergone some changes recently, and is beginning to carry really useful, thoughtful articles.

Websites

Not much out there right now, but we expect to see more in the near future (times they are a-changin'!)

http://www.michaelhyatt.com
Devoted to "self-reliant living," many excellent writers contribute frequently, including Michael Hyatt, Jim Lord, Geri Guidetti, Larry Pratt, Susan Conniry, and we do, too!

We've got a website for our magazine *Fencers Quarterly Magazine*, which includes our e-mail address if you need to contact us: http://users.townsqr.com/ale/fqm.htm

Other Books by the Evangelista's

Nick Evangelista:
The Encyclopedia of the Sword (1995)
The Art and Science of Fencing (1996)
Fighting With Sticks (1998)
The Inner Game of Fencing (2000)

Anita Evangelista:
Hidden Places, Secret Words (Editor) (1980)
Hypnosis: A Journey Into the Mind (1980)
Dictionary of Hypnotism (1991)
How to Develop a Low-Cost Family Food-Storage System (1995)
Backyard Meat Production: How to Grow All the Meat You Need in Your Own Backyard (1995)
How to Live Without Electricity — And Like It (1997)

Together:
Blood-Lust Chickens and Renegade Sheep (1999)
Country Living is Risky Business (2000)
The Woman Fencer (2000)

YOU WILL ALSO WANT TO READ:

☐ **14208 BLOOD-LUST CHICKENS AND RENEGADE SHEEP: A First Timer's Guide to Country Living, by Nick and Anita Evangelista.** Wanna get out of the rat race? Dreaming of making a move to the country? Authors Nick and Anita Evangelista moved from Los Angeles to the Missouri Ozark Mountains in 1985, with that dream in mind. This book shares their experiences with the reader and offers indispensable advice on moving back to the land. It contains real stories, real experiences, real advice and real country lore from two veterans of country living. *1999, 5½ x 8½, 177 pp, illustrated, soft cover.* **$16.95.**

☐ **14187 HOW TO LIVE WITHOUT ELECTRICITY — AND LIKE IT, by Anita Evangelista.** There's no need to remain dependent on commercial electrical systems for your home's comforts and security. This book describes many alternative methods that can help you become more self-reliant and free from the utility companies. Learn how to light, heat and cool your home, obtain and store water, cook and refrigerate food, and fulfill many other household needs without paying the power company! This book contains photographs, illustrations, and mail-order listings to make your transition to independence a snap! *1997, 5½ x 8½, 168 pp, illustrated, soft cover.* **$13.95.**

☐ **14193 BACKYARD MEAT PRODUCTION, by Anita Evangelista.** If you're tired of paying ever-soaring meat prices, and worried about unhealthy food additives and shoddy butchering techniques, then you should start raising small meat-producing animals at home! You needn't live in the country, as most urban areas allow for this practice. This book clearly explains how to raise rabbits, chickens, quail, ducks, and mini-goats and – pigs for their meat and byproducts, which can not only be consumed but can also be sold or bartered. Improve your diet while saving money and becoming more self-sufficient! *1997, 5½ x 8½, 136 pp, illustrated, soft cover.* **$14.95.**

☐ **14176 HOW TO DEVELOP A LOW-COST FAMILY FOOD-STORAGE SYSTEM, by Anita Evangelista.** If you're weary of spending a large percentage of your income on your family's food needs, then you should follow this amazing book's numerous tips on food-storage techniques. Slash your food bill by over fifty percent, and increase your self-sufficiency at the same time through alternative ways of obtaining, processing and storing foodstuffs. Includes methods of freezing, canning, smoking, jerking, salting, pickling, krauting, drying, brandying and many other food-preservation procedures. *1995, 5½ x 8½, 120 pp, illustrated, indexed, soft cover.* **$10.00.**

☐ **19206 FIGHTING WITH STICKS, *by Nick Evangelista*.** Errol Flynn, Bruce Lee, and Sean Connery did it. So did Medieval swordsmen and African warriors who wielded their oars as weapons. It's the ancient art of stick fighting, revered and explained by author Nick Evangelista. Detailed instructions guide the reader through proper attire, equipment, and sportsmanship codes for stick fighting, as a game or in self-defense. Why sticks? Because they're handy, easy to operate, and don't require ammunition or a license. In the event of a societal breakdown or near holocaust, you'd still be able to find a stick and use it. *1998, 5½ x 8½, 158 pp, illustrated, soft cover.* $15.00.

☐ **14181 EAT WELL FOR 99¢ A MEAL, *by Bill and Ruth Kaysing*.** Want more energy, more robust, vigorous health? Then you must eat food that can impart these well-being characteristics and this book will be your faithful guide. As an important bonus, you will learn how to save lots of money and learn how to enjoy three homemade meals a day for a cost of less than one dollar per meal. The book will show you how to shop, how to stock your pantry, where to pick fresh foods for free, how to cook your 99¢ meal, what foods you can grow yourself, how to preserve your perishables, several recipes to get you started, and much much more. *1996, 5½ x 8½, 204 pp, illustrated, indexed, soft cover.* $14.95.

☐ **14183 THE 99¢ A MEAL COOKBOOK, *by Ruth and Bill Kaysing*.** Ruth and Bill Kaysing have compiled these recipes with one basic thought in mind: People don't like overprocessed foods and they can save a lot of money by taking things into their own hands. These are practical recipes because they advise the cook where to find the necessary ingredients at low cost. And every bit as important — the food that you make will taste delicious! This is a companion volume to the *Eat Well for 99¢ A Meal. 1996, 5½ x 8½, 272 pp, indexed, soft cover.* $14.95.

☐ **14175 SELF-SUFFICIENCY GARDENING, Financial, Physical and Emotional Security From Your Own Backyard, *by Martin P. Waterman*.** A practical guide to organic gardening techniques that will enable anyone to grow vegetables, fruits, nuts, herbs, medicines and other useful products, thereby increasing self-sufficiency and enhancing the quality of life. Includes sections on edible landscaping; greenhouses; hydroponics and computer gardening (including the Internet); seed saving and propagation; preserving and storing crops; and much more, including fact-filled appendices. *1995, 8½ x 11, 128 pp, illustrated, indexed, soft cover.* $13.95.

☐ **17054 HOW TO BUY LAND CHEAP, Fifth Edition,** *by Edward Preston.* This is the bible of bargain-basement land buying. The author bought eight lots for a total sum of $25. He shows you how to buy good land all over the country for not much more. This book has been revised, with updated addresses and new addresses added. It will take you through the process for finding cheap land, evaluating and bidding on it, and closing the deal. Sample form letters are also included to help you get started and get results. You can buy land for less than the cost of a night out — this book shows how. *1996, 5½ x 8½, 136 pp, illustrated, soft cover.* **$14.95.**

☐ **14205 TRAVEL-TRAILER HOMESTEADING UNDER $5,000, 2nd Edition,** *by Brian Kelling.* Tired of paying rent? Need privacy away from nosy neighbors? This updated book will show how a modest financial investment can enable you to place a travel-trailer or other RV on a suitable piece of land and make the necessary improvements for a comfortable home in which to live! This book covers the cost break-down, tools needed, how to select the land and travel-trailer or RV, and how to install a septic system, as well as water, power (including solar panels), heat and refrigeration systems. *1999, 5½ x 8½, 112 pp, illustrated, soft cover.* **$10.00.**

☐ **14178 THE WILD & FREE COOKBOOK, With a Special Roadkill Section,** *by Tom Squier.* Why pay top dollar for grocery-store food, when you can dine at no cost by foraging and hunting? Wild game, free of the steroids and additives found in commercial meat, is better for you, and many weeds and wild plants are more nutritious than the domestic fruits and vegetables found in the supermarket. Authored by a former Special Forces survival school instructor, this cookbook is chock full of easy-to-read recipes that will enable you to turn wild and free food (including roadkill!) into gourmet meals. *1996, 7¼ x 11½, 306 pp, illustrated, indexed, soft cover.* **$19.95.**

☐ **17040 SHELTERS, SHACKS AND SHANTIES,** *by D.C. Beard.* A fascinating book with more than 300 pen and ink illustrations and step-by-step instructions for building various types of shelters. The emphasis is on simplicity with easy-to-use tools such as hatchets and axes. Fallen tree shelters • Indian wicki-ups • sod houses • elevated shacks and shanties • tree houses • caches • railroad tie shacks • pole houses • log cabins • and many more. One of the great classics of outdoor lore. *1914, 5 x 7, 259 pp, illustrated, soft cover.* **$9.95.**

☐ **14192 HOUSES TO GO, How to Buy a Good Home Cheap, *by Robert L. Williams.*** Now you can own that dream home that you've always yearned for — and at an affordable price! How? By following this book's tried-and-true method of purchasing a perfectly livable house that is destined for demolition, and carefully moving it to a suitable parcel of land — all for a fraction of the amount such a home would normally cost! The author has done so several times, and shares his copious knowledge. Follow the process from selecting the proper house, through choosing a mover, to revamping the resettled house. Lots of photographs, and many solid tips on how to go about owning a comfortable home inexpensively. *1997, 8½ x 11, 152 pp, illustrated, soft cover.* **$18.95.**

☐ **14185 HOW TO BUILD YOUR OWN LOG HOME FOR LESS THAN $15,000, *by Robert L. Williams.*** When Robert L. Williams' North Carolina home was destroyed by a tornado, he and his family taught themselves how to construct a log home, even though they were unfamiliar with chain-saw construction techniques. In this practical, money-saving book, he clearly explains every step of the process. By following Williams' simple procedures, you can save tens, even hundreds of thousands of dollars, while building the rustic house you've always dreamed of owning! Profusely illustrated with diagrams and over 100 photographs, this is the best log-home construction book ever written. *1996, 8½ x 11, 224 pp, illustrated, soft cover.* **$19.95.**

☐ **14133 THE HYDROPONIC HOT HOUSE, Low-Cost, High-Yield Greenhouse Gardening, *by James B. DeKorne.*** An illustrated guide to alternative-energy greenhouse gardening. Includes directions for building several different greenhouses; practical advice on harnessing solar energy; and many hard-earned suggestions for increasing plant yield. This is the first easy-to-use guide to home hydroponics. This hard-core working manual for the serious gardener is fully illustrated with diagrams, charts, and photographs. *1992, 5½ x 8½, 178 pp, illustrated, index, soft cover.* **$16.95.**

*We offer the very finest in controversial and unusual books! — A complete catalog is sent **FREE** with every book order. If you would like to order the catalog separately, please see our ad on the last page of this book.*

- 14208 Blood-Lust Chickens and Renegade Sheep, $16.95
- 14187 How to Live Without Electricity And Like It, $13.95
- 14193 Backyard Meat Production, $14.95
- 14176 How To Develop a Low-Cost Family Food-Storage, $10.00
- 19206 Fighting With Sticks, $15.00
- 14181 Eat Well for 99¢ A Meal, $14.95
- 14183 The 99¢ A Meal Cookbook, $14.95
- 14175 Self-Sufficiency Gardening, $13.95
- 17054 How to Buy Land Cheap, $14.95
- 14205 Travel-Trailer Homesteading Under $5,000, $10.00
- 14178 The Wild & Free Cookbook, $19.95
- 17040 Shelters, Shacks & Shanties, $9.95
- 14192 Houses to Go, $18.95
- 14185 How to Build Your Own Log Home, $19.95
- 14133 The Hydroponic Hot House, $16.95
- 88888 The Best Book Catalog in the World, $5.00

CLRB2

LOOMPANICS UNLIMITED
PO BOX 1197
PORT TOWNSEND, WA 98368

Please send me the books I have checked above. I am enclosing $ _____ which includes $4.95 for shipping and handling of orders up to $25.00. Add $1.00 for each additional $25.00 ordered. *Washington residents please include 7.9% for sales tax.*

NAME_____

ADDRESS _____

CITY_____

STATE/ZIP _____

We accept Visa, Discover, and MasterCard.
To place a credit card order *only,* call 1-800-380-2230,
24 hours a day, 7 days a week.
Check out our Web site: www.loompanics.com